MORE DIALOGUES IN SWING

SWING

Intimate Conversations With the Stars
of the Big Band Era

By

FRED HALL

Pathfinder Publishing of California
Ventura, CA

MORE DIALOGUES IN SWING

Intimate Conversations With the Stars of the Big Band Era

By
Fred Hall

Edited by Eugene D. Wheeler

Published By:
Pathfinder Publishing
458 Dorothy Avenue
Ventura, CA 93003
(805) 642-9278

Copyright © 1991 by Fred Hall

Library of Congress Cataloging-in-Publication Data

Hall, Fred, 1923

More dialogues in swing ; intimate conversations with the stars of the big band era / by Fred Hall.

p. cm.

Includes bibliographical references and index.

Discography: p.

ISBN 0-934793-31-X (hard cvr) : $22.95. -- ISBN 0-934793-32-8 (soft cvr) : $14.95

1. Big bands--United States. 2. Jazz musicians--Interviews. 3. Swing (Music)--History and criticism. 4. Jazz--History and criticism. I. Title

ML3518.H29   1991

781.65'4'0922--dc20   91-11466

CIP

MN

ISBN 0-934793-31-X Hard Cover

ISBN 0-934793-32-8 Soft Cover

DEDICATION

For Mike, Tim And Suli

And In Memory Of Jane

ACKNOWLEDGEMENTS

I am indebted to the many readers who so enthusiastically welcomed the original *Dialogues in Swing* and thereby made possible this volume. Thanks go as well to the interviewees who so graciously took so much of their time to talk freely and at length with me about their lives and eras. My longtime friend and associate, Bob Perry, in Santa Barbara kept my show, "Swing Thing," in circulation all over this country while I worked on this manuscript. Len Black, my representative in Europe, did likewise for that part of the world. It was most gracious of Jo Stafford and Paul Weston to write the Foreword to this book, but then they've always been known as two of the nicest people in the world of music. Especial gratitude is due to the Monte family: Pee Wee, Vi and Sal who helped so much in the verbal portrait of their boss of nearly fifty years, Harry James. Alvino and Luise King Rey supplied some valuable pictures and other material, as did Ray and Nancy Avery of Jazz Archives. Publisher-Editor Eugene Wheeler provided support and guidance without which I could not have proceeded. Most important of all those to whom I have reason to be grateful is my wife, Gita, who, with great good taste, served as first-draft editor and full-time inspiration in this as in all my other efforts.

Fred Hall

March 1991

FOREWORD

By

Jo Stafford and Paul Weston

It's a pleasure to write the foreword to Fred Hall's new book *MORE DIALOGUES IN SWING* because not only are the subjects people we've known all our musical lives, but Fred's marvelous knowledge of the business makes the interviews so informative and enjoyable.

We all have at one time or another been on a radio interview where the host sits there and makes a statement like, "Jo, you were born in Coalinga, California" and Jo has the choice of saying "Yes, I was" or launching off on her own into some other area. In contrast, Fred always has a provocative question ready which stimulates the interview and makes the artist feel at ease.

The artists in this volume cover just about every facet of the pop music business and each one has had a very interesting career.

Reading Herb Jeffries' comment about the Duke Ellington band reminded Paul that around 1932, when he was playing clarinet and piano and arranging for the Dartmouth band, he copied Duke's recording of *Sophisticated Lady*, with that incredible saxophone chorus led by Johnny Hodges. He had the chutzpa to adapt it for the seven-piece band. Much later, after Jo and Paul were married, Jo remembered that, at the very same time, she and her classmates at Long Beach High would make a ritual of playing that same Ellington record of *Sophisticated Lady* every morning just before classes began. It was their inspiration for the day. Then, still later, Jo got to do the "Jo Plus Jazz" album with Johnny Hodges, Ray Nance and Ben Webster, all from the Ellington band. She and Hodges did Billy Strayhorn's *Day Dream* together. Strayhorn was, of course, Duke's right-hand man, co-composer and arranger. After the track was made, Jo overheard Hodges say to Webster, "Hey, Billy would have loved that performance." It was a big thrill for her. What wonderful memories this book brings back.

Les Brown and Paul have been golf and bridge partners for over thirty years, and Les has never stood up in front of anything but a fine band.

At Hollywood parties in the '40s and '50s David Rose and Paul were sort of the "warm-up" piano players until Johnny Green got there. He'd sweep into the room, push them off the piano bench and take over. Dave once remarked "Do you realize that he sometimes plays the wrong chords with more authority than we do the right ones?"

And finally we must echo Tony Bennett's characterization of Johnny Mercer as "American's greatest poet—an astounding talent—true Americana." It only takes one trip through John's catalogue to show that he was the one lyricist who wrote every type of song—ballad, jazz dixie, love song, show tune, blues— you name it. He was an American classic in every category.

You'll enjoy *MORE DIALOGUES IN SWING*. These are fine people and Fred Hall enables them to tell their stories in a truly entertaining manner.

Jo Stafford and Paul Weston

TABLE OF CONTENTS

INTRODUCTION

This book is intended for **all** of those who, like me, were lucky enough to have grown up during one of the most genuinely musical periods in history. That includes the jazz fans, the devotees of the big bands and those who romanced, married and grew to maturity serenaded by the great ballad singers of the era. I wanted to include a balance of the prestigious band leaders, the solo performers, the composers and the singers. Many are still around to delight us and new generations. I had help in making choices from hundreds of readers of the original *Dialogues In Swing* but the final decisions on interviewees was exceedingly difficult. I hope I have included some of your favorites.

The interviews, done originally for my internationally-syndicated radio show, "Swing Thing," were recorded in the home of the artist, backstage at a concert, or in my home after a performance. These were relaxed sessions and little editing was done. Some of these greats have died since the interview (Teddy Wilson, Johnny Green, Harry James). Others were best known as celebrated sidemen (Sweets Edison, Marshall Royal). Most are still vital and active. You may find some surprising, even controversial, reflections. They are all, however, honest and from the heart.

In the back of the book you will find a list of Sources, including biographies and references for deeper reading about a particular artist. There is an expanded discography, as well. I hope these and the memories and opinions of those interviewed will give pleasure to those who "were there," and expand the knowledge of those who are just joining the Golden Era now, if only in retrospect.

1

KAY STARR

$\mathbf{O}$f all the singing stars it's been my pleasure to talk with, none
has been more genuine, down-to-earth and quotable than Katherine Laverne Starks of Dougherty, Oklahoma. We know her
and love her as Kay Starr. Over a number of years I've interviewed Kay and found her effervescent and totally at ease. Some
people think of her as a pop-singer, a maker of hits like *Side By
Side* and *Rock and Roll Waltz*. Others point to Kay's country
hits, like *Bonaparte's Retreat*. To me, she was and is a jazz artist
with roots in country. She was nurtured by the greatest of the
jazz violinists, Joe Venuti, and got her B.A. with Bob Crosby,
Glenn Miller and Charlie Barnet. Her first solo records were
strictly jazz and she has recorded with jazz masters whenever
possible.

Touching bases with her when I wrote this, Kay told me, "I
do just about what I want to do when I want to do it. I don't have
to work if I don't want to and I'm picking and choosing and
having a real good time. I always wanted to sing with Woody
Herman's band and I just finished a tour of my own with Woody
Herman's orchestra. If I work this out just right I'll get to sing
with every band I ever wanted to sing with. They may all be

"ghost" bands, but the book is the same and the feel and the flavor. We had Buddy DeFranco and "The Four Freshmen!" Kay had been spending part of her time in Honolulu and part in Los Angeles until she recently got a divorce and, "sold the house in Honolulu and made a whole lot of money and I'm a single lady, happy to report, and everything worked out just fine!"

FRED: Kay, you are like a number of other people I've talked with. Peggy Lee started on a radio station in the Dakotas, Dinah Shore in New York, Sinatra in New York, Rosemary Clooney on WLW in Cincinnati and I think you were on what, WRR in Dallas?

KAY: WRR in Dallas, WHBQ, WMC, WREC, that was in Memphis, so I started in both places.

FRED: Those were golden days — people don't remember live radio.

KAY: No.

FRED: These were sustainers weren't they, 15 minutes?

KAY: Yes, I had a 15-minute show five days a week. On Saturday we did a thing called the Saturday Night Jamboree which was all country. I mean it's called country today—it was hillbilly then—that shows you how far back I go. But I was one of the first ones to ever tap dance on radio.

FRED: Holy smoke. Was that in Dallas or Memphis?

KAY: That was in Memphis. Somebody brought it up, you know. People on a country show—they're just folksy as can be. They started talking about this and they called me "the kid" because I was the youngest one on the show. And they said, "Well, you know the kid here tap dances." Well, that's all the listeners had to hear. They couldn't see me, but, boy, they wanted it proved that I could tap dance. So when I came the next Saturday they had one of those roll-out sort of dance floor things—it wasn't very big. They had a pair of tap shoes and they insisted that I tap dance on the radio, so I did. Shoot, ignorance is bliss—they told you to do it, you did it.

FRED: How did you happen to get into show business at all? I understand you were at the tender age of nine?

KAY: Well, I sang all the time and my mother and dad, they enjoyed it, you know. They thought it was cute and I entertained their friends and my friends. But I had an aunt who, I guess had a business sense about her. She said to my mother, "Let's put her on an amateur show." She said, "My God, Nora, we can't do that, she's just a kid." She said, "Well, I know, but she's good—let's put her on there." So finally she broke my mother down and made a deal with her. She said, "If she does good she's yours, if she does bad she's mine." And, you know, you can't fight a deal like that, so I went on this amateur hour in Dallas, Texas, and won. Didn't win much. I won third place, not first place. I won a little plastic thing that looked like a beer mug and it had those little things and you blew on them and it says, "How dry I am"—that and free tickets for the next Saturday. But that was a start.

So after that my aunt was absolutely drunk with power and she insisted and insisted and finally there was another amateur hour that had to do with the radio. You didn't win anything except a chance to stay over for the next show and to compete with the next group of children that were gonna come in. And I kind of started winning that and they talked about me because I looked like the Pillsbury Dough Boy. Up until I was about 17 or 18 years old when I was singing with Bob Crosby's band I still weighed 165 pounds, so I was no light weight and when I was 12 or 13 years old I weighed 150, 160 pounds.

FRED: Hard to believe, looking at you now.

KAY: Well, baby fat—they can talk about it all they want to, but when do you stop being a baby? I mean some of us are still babies, you know, as far as the fat's concerned, but it's been a struggle all my life. And people, like Italians think I'm Italian and Greeks think I'm Greek and Irish think I'm Irish and . . .

FRED: You do have some Irish in you, don't you?

KAY: Yes.

FRED: And what, Indian?

KAY: Yeah, American Indian and Irish. It's marvelous because the Latin people, they like their women zaftig, so I didn't really have any trouble with Italians or Latins or Greeks. They thought, "Boy, she's just the right size." Boy, I was dying, though.

FRED: In Memphis, then, a famous fiddle player came along.

KAY: Yes, yes—Joe Venuti. I spoke to Joe about two weeks before he passed on and he was still very much alert. He couldn't believe that I had called him, but it took me forever to find him.

FRED: Well, he was supposed to be the greatest practical joker of all time, Joe Venuti.

KAY: Oh, he gave me one rule, Fred, that I guess I've lived by and it says, "If you're gonna make a mistake, make it so loud everybody else sounds wrong." That's why I think I sing so loud, I really do. That man gave us a sense of importance within ourselves because when we found out that we could bluff our way through something, whether we knew what we were doing or not, that gives us a lot of confidence. But I tell you, that fiddle bow stings when he hits you from behind. If you just even hesitate he swats you one and says, "Uh, uh." And we had to keep going, and by God, we all grew up with that. And I'm thankful for it myself. I think if I had any style or anything that is different, I think I can probably attribute it to Joe Venuti. First of all his good taste in music and mostly because he did give me assurance in myself.

FRED: He had a big band at that time, didn't he, a touring band of what, 12, 14 . . .?

KAY: Yeah. Fourteen, fifteen musicians. And it was kind of sad because I would sing with him only in the summer time because that was the only time I was out of school. But he came to the Claridge Hotel where I was doing this 50 minute show five days a week. And his road manager, Elmer Beechler, I will never forget that man's name. He heard me and again, he didn't know whether I was a kid or whether I wasn't. He just heard the voice, and with the fact that I was a local girl, boy, that really sounded good. And the contracts called for him to have a girl singer. Well, he got there and he didn't have one and they were just raising hell with him so he had to get a girl singer quick or he was not gonna get to open. So this seemed like it was just ideal. So they called me and I didn't know how to deal with it. I'd never had anybody offer me a job like that. Up to this point nobody had really offered me any money. Everything was like, you know, the barter system—you do this for me and I'll do that for you and there really wasn't too much money exchanged anywhere along the line up to this point. He wanted to talk to me about joining the band and I said, "Oh, well, you're gonna have to talk to my family." And he says, "What do you mean, talk to your family?" I said, "Well, I'm fourteen and a half years . . ." He says, "Oh, my dear, oh, wait a minute." He got nervous as could be and he says, "Well, let me call you back."

So I didn't think anything about it. I told my mother and dad about it but then he did call the radio station and they gave him my home number and he called my folks and said, "I wonder if I could talk to you." Now it got even sweeter, you know, as it went along. We got a local girl. We get to play the date because we got a girl singer. She's local, fourteen and a half years old, my God, and she sounds like she could be twenty. I mean it just got to be better and better—it's getting to be a soap opera. So they really wanted to have me on that bandstand until they got a look at me. Then they didn't know if I'd fit on the bandstand. But then, of course, Joe loved it because Joe was round, too. So it made two round people on that bandstand. I was scared to death for the longest time, but Joe got me over that because he was so sweet and so nice and so kind to me. And, of course, I was home and that helped a lot too. So I had a lot to overcome, but didn't realize it was a lot because I had help.

FRED: And your mother went with you, probably, when you were on tour.

KAY: When I went in the summer time, yes. But my father told Joe, he says, "At twelve o'clock she comes off that bandstand, I don't care if she's in the middle of a word—she comes off the bandstand." Because I went to school and oh, I tell you, I was big stuff in school, you know, singing with the orchestra at the Claridge Hotel. Joe and Sally Venuti took me in like I was their own. I always had an adjoining room to theirs and I never was afraid and I always felt like I was with family.

FRED: Joe got you with Glenn Miller?

KAY: No, Joe talked me into going this one summer. I did it all in one summer and this was like the last summer that I sang with Joe. And we had been on the road and I was used to Joe, used to everything that he did. And all of a sudden we get this call from the Bob Crosby Orchestra. They wanted a girl singer for the Chesterfield Supper Club. Well, he talked to Joe about it—the manager, the road manager or whoever it was from the Crosby band. Joe told him, "Well, you know, she's kind of young, she's in her teens." And they said, "Well, that's okay, we want her for the show. We may do a few one-nighters, but mostly it will be for the radio show." And so Joe says, "Well, let me talk to her."

Well, when Joe told me what had happened and that they wanted me and that he wanted me to go, I thought he was trying to get rid of me. Oh, I cried. It broke my heart. I was comfortable where I was and I hated the idea of growing up and taking another step. But he convinced me that if I was going to be a singer of any stature at all, I could not stay treading water where I was. So reluctantly my mother and I packed up and we left and we met the band in Detroit. I wish you could have seen their faces when I stepped off that train. I mean all of me stepped off that train. The saving grace was that they gave me all of the ballads, the unrequited love and the songs that told stories. They had another girl named Dorothy Claire who wore great Skeezix. Do you remember those Skeezix curls?

FRED: Sure. I remember Dorothy Claire.

KAY: Well, she had a Skeezix curl in front and a great big bow to match. Every dress that she had had a bow that matched it. And she did all the boop, boop, ditum, dotum, watum, shoo songs. So you know, I wasn't expected to cover the spectrum. I just did my thing and went back over and sat down in my chair when we did do any kind of dates at all. That was okay. I did that and then when I finished with the Chesterfield Supper Club we went back to the Plymouth Hotel in New York City. My mother had never seen the Automat and she wanted to see money go in and the pie come out, you know, that kind of thing. Oklahoma, Texas, and Tennessee didn't have anything like that and she wanted to see it. So we were gonna stay a couple of days and kind of walk up and down Broadway and see what we'd read about—always we're reading about it.

The first day we were back there we got a call and it was from the road manager of the Glenn Miller band and I thought, "Oh, somebody's playing a joke on me—Glenn Miller—me, how did he ever hear about me?" Well, he really seemed to be serious and he said, "I'd like to talk to you." Of course, my mother, mid-Victorian that she was—we had a room with a bed and a dresser and a bathroom—you don't receive men in your bedroom. I said, "Listen, why don't you talk to my mother." He was still sputtering when I put her on and I'm still saying, "talk to my mother," because now I'm seventeen, you know, or sixteen and a half. So she gets on the phone with him and we go down into the lobby and we talk. He kind of laughs because he says, "Look, we just want you for about eight or ten days." I kept pulling on my mother's dress because I really wanted to do it. Could you imagine? Sixteen and a half and I could sing with Glenn Miller? It's like dying and going to heaven ahead of time. So that was how all of that came about.

I sang at the Glen Island Casino for, oh, eight, nine days. That was the first recording that I made with a big band—*Baby Me* and *Love With a Capital U.* And the fun thing on that, which I didn't know about at the time, was that we had no arrangements or anything. I sang only standards. People like Chummy

McGregor and Irving Fazola, and all those guys that were on the band liked the sound they heard but could not believe that I was sixteen and a half years old because heavy people look older. They thought that and then with the sound that I had they knew I drank bathtub gin. They just knew that. And so they started playing games with me. And I didn't know what they were doing. I'd start in one key and the next eight bars they would go into another key. They just kept going and I just kept going with them because I didn't know any different. I thought, "Well, aren't they the nicest guys, making me an arrangement."

They were trying to trap me, see, and I didn't know it. The guys in the band loved me because they realized that I didn't know what I was doing, but it came so naturally that it was sheer joy for them to play with me. Of course, the people dancing out there that were trying to sing the song with me couldn't figure out what in the world was going on. They thought, "Well, it can't be bad, it's gotta be right, Glenn Miller's doing it." I gained a lot of friends at that early age because of the natural ability to just be able to do the transitions with them when they did it.

FRED: That must have been an all too brief experience, though. You were filling in for Marion Hutton, were you?

KAY: Yeah, for Marion Hutton. She was in the hospital. And I did the two songs and they were too high for me, but again, I didn't know anything about arranging. I didn't even know about keys. They'd say, "Start singing." And I'd start singing. They'd say, "Okay, try it in this key."

FRED: They had been arranged for Marion?

KAY: They had been arranged for her ahead of time. When I listen to them now I just die laughing because I really sound like a jazzed up Alfalfa. You know, reaching for those high notes. But I was gonna make them because it was that important to me.

FRED: Those were pretty exciting records, though, and especially the air check versions of them that are available.

KAY: Oh, I tell you, the thing that thrilled me . . . at my age now, when I can look back I appreciate it. I just wish I would have been a little bit older so that I could have appreciated it more. But if I had been a little bit older then I'd have been a whole lot older now, so I don't want to fool with that. I'm gonna leave things alone the way they are now. But in any case, when they put out the commemorative album for Glenn Miller they put those two little rotten songs in there and that made me so proud.

FRED: You went back to school after that?

KAY: Yeah, I had to go back and finish high school, sure. But then after that Joe and Sally had told my parents, they really had a talk with them and said, "Now look, she cannot stay in Memphis." We didn't have any recording studios. We didn't even have Elvis Presley—we didn't have anything. We just had West Memphis, Arkansas, which is where you could get drinks. But other than that we just didn't really have much in Memphis. We had the Memphis Cotton Carnival once a year, but that's like waiting for summer vacation. You just gotta wait 'till it's time. He said, "If she's going to be a singer, she's got to be out there where people can hear her. She's got to be out there where she can learn things. She's got to be out there where she can record. She's gotta do all these things."

The last year I was in high school was like when the bands, the war was on, and the bands were getting less and less because the musicians were being drafted. The ones that weren't being drafted for the service itself were going into the service bands. The few good musicians that were left were playing with the A-number-one top bands. So a couple of times Joe just decided he wasn't gonna have it because we'd end up with girl trombone players and girl bass players and that has to hurt somebody with the quality of training that Joe had had all his life and the quality of music that he wanted to produce, even on a one-nighter. I mean it must have just gone against the grain something terrible. Of course it was a lark for all of us kids because everybody in the band was not over 22 years old.

FRED: Tell me a little bit about those years with the Charlie Barnet band.

KAY: During the war when we played the theater in New York, we couldn't get laundry done because we were doing one-nighters. So I'd say, "Okay, you guys, I don't want to be down-wind of you—God, you smell." And they'd say, "Well, you know, Kay, we can't get . . ." And I said, "I'll tell you what you do. You take that shirt home tonight and you wash it and you bring it back here. Bring it back thirty minutes early and I'll press the collar, down the front, and the cuffs and up to your elbow." And that's what I used to do, and they used to smell a whole lot better. I'd hold their money for them when they'd get paid, because they knew they were gonna go out and get drunk and probably get rolled. I was sometimes carrying, I could be carrying so much money I couldn't go anyplace myself.

FRED: How did you get with Capitol Records?

KAY: Well, I did volumes of jazz for Gene Norman and Dave Dexter and all of those people and they were on the Capitol label if you remember. And they became conscious of me. I guess I did so many volumes of it and so many jazz concerts and so many things like that, but I did it step by step. I didn't go in because with Capitol, you know, they had every big girl singer there was. I guess Helen O'Connell is the only big girl singer they didn't have and she was singing with Jimmy Dorsey's band. That's why they didn't have her. But they had every other girl singer. A girl singer they did not need. So I went from the jazz to the purple label. And the purple label was like royalty. That was where all the top girl singers were. I think it was during the time when they were gonna have a musician's strike. So they decided that they would do a number of records with me just to cover things, you know. They asked me to make a list of songs that I might like to record. Well, I didn't do anything but standards. I didn't do any of the new songs—nobody ever asked me to do any of those so I didn't have any call for them. I kept handing these lists in and I kept getting these lists back with lines going through all the songs. Well, I couldn't understand it. And they didn't offer any—they just said, "Well, we got a lot of singers and a lot of people recording and we're trying to get them all double and triple and quadruple dates so that we can be covered." And that made sense to me. I sure didn't want to make any waves in the water—I was so glad they wanted me to record at all. So I said, "Well, okay, I got some more songs." So I went back and, boy, it was getting closer and closer and they were getting panicky, but what was happening was, they were having to hand these lists to Peggy Lee, Jo Stafford, Margaret Whiting, Ella May Morse—did I miss anybody?

FRED: Martha Tilton.

KAY: Well, all of them. And if they saw a song they said, "Hey, that looks like a good song." They'd mark it. I was getting their songs for them and I didn't know it, see. So I was just heartbroken because they said, "You gotta get it and you gotta get it right now." Well, I didn't know what I was gonna do because I knew if I handed in another list of songs I was probably gonna get another list with all the names crossed off again. I'm by nature a very happy sort of person, but I'm telling you, you'd have thought my whole family had been wiped out by the way I felt inside. It showed on my face. I went down—do you remember that little hangover club they had down there? Red Nichols worked there. I used to go down there a lot because I knew I could go in there by myself and nobody would bother me because the guys at the band would see to it.

I'd sit back with the wives and listen to the band. I went down there this night and they didn't serve anything but hamburgers. You could get drinks—all the kinds of drinks you wanted, but all they served was a hamburger in a basket. Well, of course, that was my favorite meal anyway. So I went down there to eat my supper and to listen to the band. I went early and the band just came in and they're setting up and Red came over and said, "My God," he says, "Who died?" I said, "Well, I guess you could say I died, because my record career's going down the drain." He said, "What do you mean?" I told him what had happened and he says, "Well, you wait. I'm gonna come over at intermission; we're gonna talk."

If it were not for Red Nichols I guess I would not have a career with Capitol Records. He said, "I can fix their buns real fast." Of course he didn't use the word, buns. And he says, "I'm gonna come get you tomorrow and we're gonna go to my garage." He says, "You always hear about those piano benches that's got music in them." He says, "Well, I got one that's got music in it." He says, "And we're gonna get those songs out." And he got out all these songs that I started with: *Mama Goes Where Papa Goes, Poor Papa, You Gotta See Your Mama Every Night,* all those songs where the sheet music had all those ladies that had the spit curls, you know. If it had not been for him . . . And I tell you, I made out that list and when I got it back it didn't have a mark on it—they didn't know any of those songs. So if it had not been for Red I guess I would not have had any career at all with the recording and certainly not with Capitol.

FRED: Did any one of those that you did hit?

KAY: Yes, *Lonesomest Gal In Town* hit, but it hit locally. It just hit locally and then . . . I still get requests for *Mama Goes Where Papa Goes* and things like that—it's rare, but I get it from time to time.

FRED: Capitol was a prolific recording studio. Every month just dozens of great albums came out . . .

KAY: Well, even when I got on the Capitol purple label, I still was fighting for my life because I was still in there with all these girls. I didn't have any problems when they wanted somebody to sing with Ernie Ford, because Peggy Lee wouldn't sing and Ella May Morse didn't sing that way and Margaret Whiting wasn't gonna sing that way, so who was left? Katherine Laverne Starks. So they asked me if I'd sing with him. Well, I started out singing hillbilly and country and stuff so it appealed to me. And thank God it did. We had a very good song there with Ernie and me with *I'll Never Be Free.* But always I was fighting for every step of the way. And we had the A & R people who were always looking for songs for us, but some of the best songs that I had, they didn't find for me—I found "Bonaparte's Retreat" myself.

FRED: That was what, out of a . . . That's a country song . . .

KAY: Yeah, that's a country song. It belongs to Roy Acuff and I found it in Dougherty, Oklahoma, where I was born. The biggest building there is the depot. You know, Oklahoma for a long, long time was dry and they had three-and-two beer and you could drink a lot of it—you didn't get drunk, ever.

FRED: You got fat.

KAY: You got fat and you knew the way to the bathroom. You knew that well. But other than that, you know, there wasn't anything there. But I heard this song and it was a fiddle song and I just loved it. I asked the man when the night was over if I could take it out of the machine and see who the publishers were. I figured that way I could find out about the song. And sure enough it was Roy Acuff and I called him from Mrs. Sibley's Grain Store—that was the only phone we had in town—I mean this was a little town. Of course, my mother lives in Sulfur now which is nine miles from there and Ardmore which is a big town nineteen miles from Sulfur. We're stepping up in the world—it's taken us a while, but we're getting there.

But I went to Mrs. Sibley's Grain Store and called him and I told him I wanted to record the song and he said, "Why, that's wonderful, go ahead on." And I said, "Well, it was a fiddle song." He said, "But that's okay." I said, "No, it's not okay, I don't play fiddle." He says, "Oh, well what do you play?" I said, "I don't play nothing, I'm a singer." And I said, "Are there any lyrics to it?" "Oh," he says, "Wait a minute, wait a minute, hang on." And he says, "You know something, I just asked them and they said we don't have no words to that song."

And I guess he could feel the disappointment over the phone and he says, "You a singer, huh?" I said, "Yes, and I just love that song." I said, "You don't have no words?" And he says, "No, we don't have no words." He says, "But now you just wait a minute." And he says, "Listen, you sound like you want to sing

13

that song. If you want to sing it and you like it that much . . . you called me long distance, by God, this is your nickel—we're gonna make you up some words." And they did and that's turned out to be *Bonaparte's Retreat*.

FRED: Right then and there.

KAY: Yeah. Mm hm.

FRED: Holy smoke. *Side by Side* was a departure, wasn't it? Wasn't it the first record where a singer sang with herself?

KAY: Yeah, yeah.

FRED: Was that Dave's idea or yours?

KAY: Well, it was kind of Hal Stanley's and mine. Hal Stanley would love for everybody to have been back in vaudeville days. He loved the old jokes and the old songs and *Side by Side*. He says, "You know, that ought to be a soft shoe." I said, "Stanley, it is a soft shoe." And he says, "Well, it ought to feel like a soft shoe." And he would go through all these gyrations and I said, "Well, why don't we do, you know, like a *Me and My Shadow* kind of singing." And so he says, "That's it—that's it." So we started working. We worked and we worked and we worked with Hal Mooney and a few people like that because I don't read music and Hal Stanley didn't read music, so it was like the blind leading the blind. We needed somebody to help us put it all together, but we had the thought. We took it in and they loved it and since then it's caught on with a lot of people, but we were the first.

FRED: You've got to explain who Hal Stanley is to our audience.

KAY: Well, Hal Stanley died about a year and half ago, but Hal Stanley was my manager. He was a fellow who thought I was the best singer in the whole wide world, but he owned all these night clubs down on Central Avenue. He was T Bone Walker's best friend, Bill Basie's best friend. All those kind of people were his kind of people. When I had Stanley as my manager I inherited all these people which I am so proud and pleased with until this day.

FRED: Of all of your albums, the one I love best is the one with Basie.

KAY: Oh, that was a dream come true. I went in with this new recording contract and they said to me, "What do you want to do?" I said, "What do you mean, what do I want?" "What have you always wanted to do that you've never been able to do?" I said, "You won't let me do it." And they said, "Well, we're asking you." I said, "You mean to tell me if I tell you what I want to do, that you're gonna let me do it?" They said, "If it's possible." And don't you know that they did. Bill Basie and I had always . . . because when Stanley and I bought the Cotton Club, Bill Basie was our house band, and after everybody had gone home I used to go up there. Bill only liked to play in two keys, you know, and I don't sing in either one of them.

FRED: Fortunately one of them is C.

KAY: Yeah, I only sing a few songs in the key of C. But we used to do the blues and we used to always laugh and talk. Bill Basie talks, I say, in shorthand. I mean one word speaks volume for him and it's a marvelous way to be and he's not changed even today. And he says, "We're gonna make an album." I said, "Great." He says, "When?" I said, "Well, I don't know, you get it on." He says, "We'll get it on." And this went on for years. He'd say, "Now?" I'd say, "No." He'd say, "Later." It was always "now, no, later" for years and years and years. So they said, "Bill Basie, Count Basie?" And I said, "Yes, This has been a wish that we both have had for so many years that I think that he would do it with me." They said, "Well, I don't know. You know, he's a free agent and since he's been doing all that stuff with Frank Sinatra and . . ." And I said, "Call him and see—I think he'll do it with me." And do you know, it's the first time with Crescendo Records . . . Wasn't that the . . .?

FRED: It was Dot or one of those.

KAY: One of those. But the person that called him said, "It's the first time I've heard him use a whole sentence." He said, "I'd be very happy to—when?" So that was it. And we did it and I went to New York and I made a . . . See I have preconceived notions how I want to do songs. I've had a lot of really big band leaders and people who make arrangements say to me, "You know, it's strange working with you—usually I make the arrangement and where there's a hole the girl sings, but with you, you sing and where there's a hole the band plays." And I said, "Well, we just got to figure out whose record is this—yours or mine?" And I said, "If it's my record then I'm gonna sing and then, when I want to take a breath, that's your turn." But it's a style that I sing and sometimes it carries over into another phrase and I can't let the band be playing there if I'm gonna be singing there because there'll be cat and dog fight. So they've learned that, you know, most arrangers say, "Okay, she's got her own ideas—she's not gonna make any mistakes—she knows what she's doing." Which is a marvelous compliment to me.

FRED: My absolute favorite track of all time with you was *I Get The Blues When It Rains* from that album and *God Bless The Child* and *Keep Smiling At Trouble*.

KAY: I don't think there's a song in there I dislike.

FRED: How did *Wheel of Fortune* come about? I see on your wall you've got a gold record there.

KAY: Yes, Capitol Records. And they called me and got me up out of a sound sleep. We were covering the record that they were making in New York. I don't really understand, but as I told you before, I do not read music and I had to learn the song before we could get a key on it. So when I tell you that I quick dressed and quick got in the car and quick got to the studio, because they had the arranger there, the copyist there and the musicians were gonna come in after their gig. And I didn't know the song nearly as well as I should have known it to record it. But I had a shaking hands acquaintance with it and I liked the song. I mean I didn't fall madly in love with it the first time I heard it. How do you do that when they wake you up out of a sound sleep and there's so much . . . I mean it was like a war going on in that studio. This guy was arranging it and throwing the music in the air. They had gofers going around collecting music, handing it to the different copyists, and collecting it and a proofreader over here doing this and the musicians trailing in. We only did one song—we finished the arrangement, the copying, the recording and everything in two and a half hours.

FRED: Holy smoke.

KAY: You betcha. And we had to do it that way because if we hadn't we wouldn't catch up with them in New York where they were three hours ahead of us, you see. But I've always felt very, kind of, not very bad, but kind of bad about it because the girl that was recording it in New York, it was her chance to be a big star and it was my first crack at being a big star on record. And there, but for the grace of God, could have been this young lady if she'd been with Capitol. My claim to fame is that I was with a bigger record company so therefore we had better distribution, probably, and a lot of things, but I don't blame her for being hot.

FRED: They rushed you to the market.

KAY: You betcha, and she's still mad at me, I'm told.

FRED: Kay, you seem like a happy gal, beautiful, just living here in Bel Air. And I agree with my wife, who says you look slim, very slim.

KAY: Your wife is so dear to have you say that.

FRED: No, but it's true.

KAY: No, I'm not slim. I'm not slim, but I'm working on it. I'm working on it, but I've been working on that since the year one.

17

KAY STARR, the glamour girl.
The mischievous streak shows through.

2

COUNT BASIE

MEMORIES OF THE MAN AND THE BAND

**With Sweets Edison, Marshall Royal, Leonard Feather,
Sammy Nestico, Neal Hefti, Frank Foster**

There have been many biographical pieces written about William Basie of Red Bank, New Jersey. This is not one of them. For that kind of reading I recommend his autobiography, written with Albert Murray, *Good Morning Blues*. In what follows you'll find a surprisingly wide-range of opinion about Count Basie and his band, which is still roaring away today, under the leadership of saxophonist-arranger Frank Foster. Besides interviewing Foster, I chose sessions with trumpet-master Harry "Sweets" Edison, who joined Basie in 1938, all-round reed man Marshall Royal, who re-built the band in 1951, pre-eminent jazz critic Leonard Feather, writer of copious (and valuable) liner-notes for Basie albums, and Basie arrangers, Neal Hefti and Sammy Nestico.

It's virtually impossible, I've found, to discover whether Basie the **man**, or the **collective personnel** of the Basie band, contributed most to the Basie mystique. Sweets Edison says that Bill

Classic photo of COUNT BASIE in the peak years
of the 1960s. (Ray Avery photo)

Basie, "was the greatest band leader who ever lived." Marshall Royal's view is, "You never knew that Basie was the boss. His men made him." The Count Basie band has **always been,** as Frank Foster puts it, "the most explosive force in jazz." That was true in the earliest days in Kansas City when Basie would work out ideas on the piano and Eddie Durham would put them on paper to set the style. It was still true in 1990, when the arrangements were as important as the soloists. To me, every Basie band, even the short-lived small group of 1950, has been the absolute essence of "swing."

I think you'll discover that Count Basie had some very special things going for him. Probably the most important was the financial support and unrelenting promotional efforts of John Hammond who first heard the band on the radio from Kansas City and got it its first and subsequent recording contracts. Hammond then was a major force in choosing sidemen, getting the band established in New York and setting up good management. Willard Alexander managed the band and booked it through all those years when other bands rose and fell in this toughest of businesses. Basie, himself, was able to find a number of key band members who were natural and willing organizers and detail men. Finally, and most-importantly after 1950, came the arrangers.

The band had some fortuitous record contracts, too, from the essential (although poorly-paying) Decca days, through Columbia, Victor, Roulette and Pablo, with many shorter-lived associations along the way. Count Basie died on April 26, 1984. It's amazing how much Basie remains in the catalogues and has been reissued on CDs. Ninety-three were listed in the Fall 1990 Schwann CD catalog, the latest of which was recorded in 1989, five years after its founder died. This Denon release is properly called *The Legend, The Legacy*. Some interviews occurred before and some after Basie's death. My anecdotal overview of that legend begins with Sweets Edison, who came out of Columbus, Ohio, by way of St. Louis to New York City to play trumpet with the Lucky Millinder band. This interview with Sweets took place in 1981.

Sweets Edison

SWEETS: When I rejoined Lucky as a trumpet player, Bobby Moore in Basie's band got ill, and Jo Jones, and Walter Page said, "Man, why don't you get Sweets?" So I went and tried out for Basie's band. We went up to the Woodside (Hotel) and fortunately they liked me. So I joined Count Basie's band.

FRED: They married you. You were there awhile.

SWEETS: I'm still there. Still there in spirit. I'll go back anytime. That's home to me, Count Basie's band. He is the greatest band leader that's ever lived so far as I'm concerned. Basie's band was primarily based on solos because he had one of the most influential trumpet players who ever lived, Lester Young (Prez), and he had Buck Clayton. Why, everybody in there was a soloist, Jo Jones, Walter Page. Basie was a soloist himself.

FRED: Mostly head arrangements.

SWEETS: Nothing but head arrangements. So consequently we didn't have a limit to the length of solos that you'd play because Basie would play a certain little thing on the piano and say, "This is what I want on it." The brass section would go to a room in the Woodside and figure out the introduction, and the saxophone players, they'd go to the basement in the Woodside.

FRED: Now, the Woodside, this is before. . .?

SWEETS: It was a hotel, this was a hotel! We only had three trumpets, Buck Clayton, Ed Lewis and myself, and two trombones, which was Dan Minor and, ah, (this was before Dicky Wells) Benny Morton.

FRED: Was Freddie Green with the band?

SWEETS: Freddie Green was with the band before me. I think he joined the band in '36.

FRED: And still right there.

SWEETS: Yeah. He joined the band in 1936.

HARRY "SWEETS" EDISON (Ray Avery photo)

FRED: And you joined the band in the middle of 1938. The band hung out and rehearsed at the Woodside, but where did they play? What were the venues for the band in those days?

SWEETS: There weren't really any locations for bands to play in those days. The only choice you had was to go on the road and that was what you looked forward to, really. They had four theaters in the East which were the Apollo Theater, and you'd go to the theater in Philadelphia, the Nixon Grand, and then you'd go to Baltimore at the Royal Theater and Washington at the Howard, and from then on it was one-nighters until you'd do all the West, Midwest and South. All through there. Then coming back you'd do the Regal Theater through Chicago and then you would head for Ohio, Indiana, you know.

FRED: You were all kids in those days..

SWEETS: Yeah.

FRED: It didn't hurt the way it might have.

SWEETS: No, no! We looked forward to it. It was fantastic. I wouldn't trade those days. There's no experience like a youngster when you get with a bunch of guys. You learn to be unselfish. There is a certain amount of brotherly love that you acquire being with a band a long time, you know. You get to learn from each other. You learn how to play section work because there is quite an art in playing with the section. But nowadays they don't get that one-nighter experience. They don't get playing with different guys as an experience every night because in Basie's band we were all just like brothers in the band. Such a close knit feeling big bands had. And naturally they had the Savoy Ballroom in those days but the scale was so low. It was a regular job for about a month.

FRED: I used to go up and catch those Sunday. . .

SWEETS: Matinees?

FRED: Yeah, and the battle of the bands.

SWEETS: And those were the great days.

FRED: Something else!

SWEETS: Oh, you could hear some music. That was just like going to see a prize fight. Everybody wanted to go in to hear what band was going to play more, or what band was going to swing more. Who was going to introduce a new singer or something like that. It was just good times, you know.

FRED: Let me talk about the Decca Records a little. I don't know why it didn't cramp your style to have to tailor everything to three minutes. You were talking about being able to stretch out with solo, but the band sounds spontaneous and full of fun.

SWEETS: Most of it was head arrangements so you didn't have too much cutting out to do. You didn't have to delete any notes. You just delete some solos.

FRED: And Freddie Green never took a solo?

SWEETS: He used to be a good soloist.

FRED: Did he?

SWEETS: Yes, he sure did 'cause he and Charlie Christian, they were very good friends and Charlie Christian gave him an amplifier. But when Freddie Green would lay out in Basie's band to take a solo, the whole bottom would fall out because he was. . .

FRED: The solid underpinning.

SWEETS: The rhythm was set by him and Walter Page see, but there is only one Freddie Green. Freddie Green, he's the master of the guitar strumming when it comes to playing rhythm and keeping a band together.

FRED: That band was loaded with masters. Incidentally, your name appears on the title of a number of those riff tunes like, *Jive At Five*.

SWEETS: That was my tune, yeah! And *Every Tub*, that was my tune. *Sent For You Yesterday*, those were my riffs behind Jimmy Rushing. Oh, there were quite a few things I wrote with Basie's band. Everybody got a chance in that band. We had a chance to put our— whatever the riff that we started on the rehearsal, if it sounded good, Basie said, "Well, that's what we're going to do, let's make a tune out of that."

FRED: How did you come up with the titles?

SWEETS: Well, just named it anything. It didn't make any difference.

FRED: *Every Tub*. What's that?

SWEETS: *Every Tub*. That means when you stand up to play you're on your own. You know, the old saying is every tub sits on its own bottom. So that means even in real life it's up to you yourself whether you make it or not. It's every tub out here. It still exists, you know. So many things are given to you, but you got to get out and get it too, you know.

FRED: *Jive At Five*. Recorded at five?

SWEETS: No, that was a friend of mine named Dick Bach. He used to be a disk jockey in New York and he had a show that came on at five in the afternoon. So, we named it. He used that for his theme song, *Jive At Five*.

FRED: The band had to record some pretty silly things, too, along the line. Current pop tunes.

SWEETS: Well, at that time Basie wanted to create a name not only for original tunes like *One O'Clock Jump*, and *Swingin' The Blues*. We wanted to get to all the people, you know. Like a popular tune would come and he'd want to include that. Naturally, you don't want to keep playing what people, ah, wonder what you're playing. They have to come up and say "Well, what's the name of that that you just played?" They probably had heard it on the record, but a lot of things that we played at a dance, people would come and ask what the name of that arrangement was and who wrote it. So, Basie took any kind of tune that somebody, one of his friends would write, and have a little arrangement made on it to keep not only jazz fans, the people that loved to go to dances, but get some more fans too that knew the pop tunes.

FRED: I remember Jimmy Rushing doing things like *Smarty*.

SWEETS: Sure! That was a popular tune at that time, that was a popular tune. You'd be surprised at some of the dances that we would play, especially white dances, that would ask for *Smarty*. They wouldn't ask for *Swingin' The Blues*, they'd ask for *One O'Clock Jump*, naturally. But they would ask for *Smarty*. Earl Warren made a popular tune called *Emaline*, and they would ask for that. That kept the clients coming in all the time.

FRED: The other side of *One O'Clock Jump* was *John's Idea*, I think. Who was John?

SWEETS: John Hammond!

FRED: Ah, John Hammond. Who, of course, was the granddaddy of the. . .

SWEETS: Yeah, he was responsible for the resurgence of the blues because the blues had completely died out. There was nobody singin' the blues anymore. So the first concert that was a jazz concert at Carnegie Hall was John Hammond's idea.

FRED: *Spirituals To The Blues.*

SWEETS: *Spirituals To The Blues.*

FRED: That's right! You were in on it. . .

SWEETS: Yes, yes! Sure.

FRED: Lester Young, you. . .

SWEETS: Well, the whole band.

FRED: . . .the whole band. But you did some sextets.

SWEETS: Oh yeah, we did some sextets, quintets. The Kansas City Seven, you know and all that. Oh, it wasn't an entertaining band like the Jimmy Lunceford or the Cab (Calloway), you know, who had one of the most entertaining bands you could ever listen to. They had group singing. They had an entertaining band. Basie's band was a playing band. Nobody liked to sing in there anyway. You know, the group sang and everybody would really just screw it up so bad Basie would say, "Well, we won't do that." And, there was only one vocalist, that was Jimmy Rushing. Earl Warren, he sang for awhile and Helen Humes. She took Billie Holiday's place you know. So, that was their job, singing. Our job was to play.

FRED: Sure.

SWEETS: So, you know, we didn't infringe on their profession and they didn't infringe on ours.

FRED: Sounds like discipline was good in the band.

SWEETS: Yeah, because it was fun, it was fun. And where you have a lot of fun there is discipline.

FRED: No question who was the boss?

SWEETS: No, no, because you never knew that Basie was the boss. He wasn't always in the front. He'd get in the bus with us. He would never take a private car. The suffering that we went through, he went through the same thing. When I first joined the band we were making $6 bucks a night and Basie was only making $15. He didn't say "Well, I'm the boss and this is my band and you do what I tell you to do." Some of the band leaders would exert their title as the boss and they'd let everybody know it. Basie—today he's still the same.

FRED: He seemed totally effortless.

SWEETS: Yes, he was. Well, he left your responsibility up to you, the man himself. He knew your job is to play and he never fired anybody. When I left the band he'd never fired anybody.

FRED: Well, who influenced you primarily?

SWEETS: Well, I think my influence was everybody's. Every trumpet player's influence, Louis Armstrong. You can't meet a lead trumpet player anyplace—of course some of the youngsters never heard of Louis Armstrong.

FRED: I can't believe that!

SWEETS: Oh, sure. Some of the youngsters, they never heard of Duke Ellington. I did clinics at a college and some of them had never heard of Ethel Waters! They know Quincy Jones, but they've never heard of Fletcher Henderson!

FRED: Unbelievable!

SWEETS: Oh, sure. They know Quincy, they know Lalo Shifrin, they know most of the rock'n role arrangers, but they never heard of Fletcher Henderson who was very instrumental in making Benny Goodman popular. And then Jimmy Mundy.

Later Fletcher started playing piano with Benny Goodman. They never heard of Don Redman. There's a lot of the great arrangers that the youngsters have never heard of. I have a friend that teaches literature at Santa Monica City College, and she asked the students to bring in a paper on Louis Armstrong. One of the girls, the first thing she said, was, "Well, he was the first man on the moon."

FRED: That would make a good classification for the Jeopardy TV show, Louis Armstrong—Neil Armstrong. I don't think anybody's going to confuse **you** with Thomas A. Edison though and of course your real name is Harry. How did the "Sweets" nickname come about?

SWEETS: Lester Young gave me that name. I used to try to use more quality in my playing than anything else. I wanted a nice round sound with pretty vibrato and everything, so everything was sort of on the pretty side, you know, but. . .

FRED: Well, Lester Young gave you your nickname "Sweets" and Billie Holiday gave Lester his nickname which was "Prez." When World War II came around it was disastrous, of course, for the big bands who lost their top personnel. What happened with Lester? After the war he was not the same.

SWEETS: I think that was the great misfortune of Lester Young's life. The Army just completely destroyed him, completely destroyed him. He didn't want to go and I can understand why he didn't because if you have contributed your life to your instrument, playing your instrument, trying to protect it, that's all you can do. You don't know how to carry a gun, you haven't taken exercise, and built your body so you could carry that pack on your back. They should have had another area for musicians and entertainers, all of them. But when Lester went they put him in the Army.

FRED: They had him cleaning latrines, I think, that sort of thing.

SWEETS: That killed his spirit. That took all the spirit out of Prez. I think they just really destroyed him, I really do.

29

FRED: Basie broke up the band for awhile didn't he? He had a small group with Buddy DeFranco.

SWEETS: In the 50s.

FRED: Why was that? Economics?

SWEETS: Economics, Yeah, yeah. And he didn't have Freddie because he was going to try to make it without Freddie Green. But when he opened his first job, it was so empty, 'til he had to call Freddie Green to come to Chicago.

FRED: You were sort of in and out of the band then, for the next few years.

SWEETS: In 1951, when the band broke up, I started playing around New York. I just did freelance. I played with Buddy Rich most of the time, with his small band, regularly, Zoot Sims and myself. We had two horns and a piano player, and then Rocky Coluccio, Max Bennett on guitar, and Buddy on drums. So I played with him around New York and then I'd go on to Apollo with Stan Getz. I'd play around with all the guys. Then I went with Jazz At The Philharmonic for about three or four years. Then I recorded with Billie Holiday a lot, and did a lot of recording around New York. Then I got a job playing with Josephine Baker and I went on a tour with her for a couple years. In 1952 I went to California and I stayed out there. I started playing with Nelson Riddle and Frank Sinatra.

FRED: You were on the *Wee Small Hours* album, weren't you?

SWEETS: Yeah, that was the first album I made with Frank. *Wee Small Hours*, in 1955.

FRED: Great album.

SWEETS: Oh, that was **one** of the great albums. Then, I did studio work from '52 until '58. I traveled with Frank Sinatra and I did all of the recording, like with Nat "King" Cole, Margaret Whiting, oh, everybody.

Marshall Royal

AUTHOR'S NOTE:And so when the Count had to break up his big band in 1950, Sweets Edison was able to go on to other and greater things. Not all the musicians in the band were that lucky. The break-up of the band came as a shock to the music industry, but one person who was not so surprised was Marshall Royal, a veteran of the small band and big band wars since the early 1930s. He went on to make an important contribution and influence the future of the Basie band when it reorganized in 1951. This interview took place in 1989.

MARSHALL: The big band era had dropped so much that Basie couldn't afford to carry a big band. It was strictly financial.

FRED: If Basie couldn't, nobody could, I guess, in that time.

MARSHALL: I don't know. A few of the other guys were able to do it on occasion because they could demand larger skill salaries for their groups. You see, black bands didn't play the Pompton Turnpike and the Steel Pier and the jobs that paid money in the summer times which were. . .

FRED: The Glen Island Casino.

MARSHALL: The Glen Island Casino. Well, black bands didn't play those places. And it so happened that Basie had an angel when he started. He had John Hammond. That was the great white father and he carried him places where he ordinarily would have had to use the back door. So that was just a sign of the times. That was it!

FRED: The Jim Crow rule still held in the 50s?

MARSHALL: Jim Crow rule still holds forth now!

FRED: Does it, truly?

MARSHALL: This is 1989. It's almost 1990 and it still does—the only way that you can really know that is to wake up one morning and find out that you're a black guy. And then, all of a sudden everything comes before your mind, see. If you had to do that just one day you'd find out exactly what the whole thing's all about. You can't escape the fact that there is a difference between people. Any time you catch two white guys and one guy is a Christian and the other guy is an atheist, why, you've got trouble. So, what's you goin' to do?

FRED: When I was a kid in Washington, DC and wanted to hear the great black bands and musicians, I went to the Howard Theater.

MARSHALL: Washington, DC was considered as southern, below the Mason-Dixon line. So you had it there and if you ever really wanted to see pure prejudice, it was in Washington, DC, our Capital.

FRED: Absolutely.

MARSHALL: It was ridiculous. During the first 10, 15, 20 years that I went there, I wasn't able to stay in any kind of a hotel because there was only one black hotel there that was actually liveable. It was the one that was across the street from the Howard, backstage. It was only one floor, upstairs over the bar. Other than that, when we came in town with a bus, we got out of the bus and started running to the nearest home that we could find to ask the people, "Could we stay overnight?" Or if we were going to stay a week at the Howard Theater, arrange whether or not we could stay for a week there and live decent and be close to work. Everything was raw and nasty and it still is. It's only tongue in cheek now. But I'm not angry about it. I laugh at it every day.

FRED: I guess that's the philosophy that developed out of necessity, but let's hope that things are better today than they were in 1951 when you came to Bill Basie and put the big band together.

MARSHALL: That was my doing. I put it together and rehearsed his band for him. Sometimes you would have 12 to 15 arrangers there with stuff that they had written something "like" Basie. When you didn't write like Basie you brought what **you** could write and we **played** it like Basie. Basie said very little about anything. Basie would be sittin' around making out his racing form for Belmont while I was rehearsing his band for him.

FRED: Oh, he was a big man on the horses I know.

MARSHALL: I don't know if he's a big man or not! (both laughed)

FRED: Well, I mean he. . .(more laughter)

MARSHALL: He contributed.

FRED: I guess a lot of the guys were nuts on baseball too, weren't they?

MARSHALL: To a certain extent there were some guys there that **lived** baseball. We had maybe a half a dozen guys and between us we could tell you anything you wanted to know about baseball right down to the 100th of a percentage of the batting average of the leaders that particular day, or that particular night and we knew what was happening and who was going to get traded to who and where, when and why.

FRED: Was there a band team?

MARSHALL: Yeah, we had a band team.

FRED: Basie play?

MARSHALL: Nah, Basie never picked up a glove. We used to use him as a third base coach and that was only an appearance because he didn't know nuthin' about what was supposed to happen at third base. (Both laughed) Had a lot of fun though.

FRED: What was the magic of Basie though? Why did the band always sound like Basie and why did the band always have the cohesiveness and the stick-togetherness that it had?

MARSHALL: That's what everybody else has been trying to find out for years. It was a combination of a whole lot of different things and the only ones that actually knew ain't tellin'. You see, Basie didn't make. . . ah, guys would come up to you saying, "What did you ever learn from Basie when you were with the band?" I didn't learn a damn thing from Basie when I was in the band. What did he know how to teach me, see? He, Basie got his stuff from the men **in** his band. His **men** made **him**.

FRED: But he had to be discerning about that.

MARSHALL: He had to be discerning because he had an angel that kept the heavy part going, which is the money.

FRED: The money!

MARSHALL: The money, you see. He worked for some forty some odd years without a contract with his manager. All of those years he didn't even have a signed contract with Willard Alexander. When I first came to his band Basie didn't even know how to make out a payroll. He says, "Marshall, I want you to play with me and I want you to act as road manager and help me with this." I said, "Basie, I don't want to be involved in anybody else's money." I says, "Now the way you do it. I will help you and show you how to make out your payrolls and then you'll know how much money is coming in to you every week, which you haven't known for the last 30 years. See!" And he said, "Well, I guess you're right." So I'd sit down and help him make out his payrolls and go along with it. But I never wanted to be a manager or anything because sometimes the manager has to fire somebody out of the band and I never wanted to fire anybody.

FRED: I understand he **couldn't** fire anybody.

MARSHALL: He usually let guys fire themselves. When a guy just got intolerable, well, he was just automatically out, you know?

FRED: There was an ephemeral something going on there with that band that I guess was a sum total of guys like you and everybody else in it, and Basie himself.

MARSHALL: He had a group of guys working in his band that were probably some of the best writers in the business. When we started puttin' the big band together, Ernie Wilkins was sittin' there playing second alto under me and he was just a fine writer. This was when he was first getting started. We had to take that old book of his and weed it out and take a lot of the arrangements out of it. I helped him change tempos to it to keep from playing everything a flag-raiser. You got to play moods. There was a brotherhood that we had in the Basie band that was like a family. You didn't do a whole lot of saying or doing, but it just happened. This guy knew what you were gonna to be doin' and know how you think. If you come to work one night and somethin' is wrong somewhere, the guys knew what's wrong. Just like brothers in the band. All of them were siblings. It was a different world.

FRED: Everybody had a nickname in that band. Weren't you like Burgomeister or something like that?

MARSHALL: Yeah, everybody used to call me "the Burgomeister."

FRED: Why?

MARSHALL: Because I was the top gig in the band. Anytime there was anything to actually be done, I usually did it because Basie was so smooth-going and didn't want to be a part of anything. He'd be off doing somethin' else all the time, see. The biggest thing he did was collect the money and see that the guys were paid. Musically, he played his piano the way it was supposed to be. So far as the band, puttin' it together, he never did that. Even way back before I was a part of the band he always had somebody else in the band that took care of—I hear that Earl Warren used to do some things to help him. He always had a conductor or somebody to do his dirty work for him.

FRED: And yet, where would you've all been without Basie as the focal point?

MARSHALL: You wouldn't have been anywhere because you've got to have a start. You've got to have a foundation, whatever the foundation has to be. You've got to have a foundation. It just happened that it was that way. No doubt about it. It turned out good. Just like a person in the kitchen cookin' and you start out throwin' some bones in there to boil the stock and after awhile they throw a piece of cabbage in there and some peas and a couple pieces of carrots and whatever vegetables you have. And if they cook it all day, the longer they cook it the better it is and it's more seasoned. You put a little tabasco in here and a little thyme in here and a little something in there and pretty soon you have a wonderful soup. And if you cook it all day it's better than if you just cooked it for two hours.

It's like some of the Italian dressings that they have with their spaghetti and their sauces. Sometimes they started cookin' it at daybreak and they don't stop cookin' it until 6:00 o'clock that evening, just goin' slow. Well, it's the same thing with the band. The more you can get it congealed and together, the more you got goin'.

Leonard Feather

AUTHOR'S NOTE: One of those who chronicled the rise of the Count Basie band from humble beginnings in Kansas City to the peak of perfection in New York City many years later, was Leonard Feather, the critic and composer and writer who first heard Basie in the company of Louis Armstrong. This interview occurred in 1982.

LEONARD: I'd become friendly with Louis when he visited England, which is where I am from, you know. I flew to Chicago, not specifically to see him but I ran into him when he was playing at the Oriental Theater with his big band, and he said, "Well, what you doin', Pops? Why don't you come along and join us and see what it's like in America?" So I was invited to be a guest on the band bus. I hopped in the bus with the entire orchestra and we went down to St. Louis and Kansas City. And I gotta' tell you, Fred, I had never in my life experienced that kind of heat. It was one of those—this is almost before air conditioning was invented, it was that long ago, you know. You can't believe what it was like for an Englishman because, you know, for us, in London 75 degrees was a boiling hot day and it was around 110 or something. But in spite of that, I had a marvelous time hearing not only Louis's band but Andy Kirk. In Kansas City I dropped in at a small place called the Reno Club and heard an obscure 9 piece band by the name of Count Basie. It was the week after John Hammond had been there. Isn't that amazing?

FRED: And John, of course, is responsible for getting Basie out of there and to New York.

LEONARD: Right, and he was the one that got the whole thing started and I didn't know anything about it. And, Jimmy Rushing was singing and Hot Lips Page was sort of a guest soloist in the band.

FRED: This was shortly after Basie had taken over from Bennie Moten?

LEONARD: Well, yeah, within a year and a half, that's right. I really didn't know that much about him. I'd heard him on a few records of Bennie Moten's.

FRED: Any relation between the Basie Band today and the Basie Band then? Do you get any of the same feel?

LEONARD: No. I really don't think so. I think the Basie Band today is a very smooth, well organized machine with fine arrangements, some fine soloists. But to tell the truth, this sounds heretical, but I heard Juggernaut a couple of weeks ago at the Concord Jazz Festival and they sounded more like the old Basie Band with that loose, you know, swinging feel, than the Basie Band itself today does.

I'm not putting down the Basie Band today, it's just two different kinds of feelings. But when Nat Pierce and Frank Capp and that band, which includes some Basie alumni of course, when they play one of those old Basie things like *Moten Swing* you really get that feeling of the old Basie Band, whereas Basie today isn't playing *Moten Swing* very much, if at all. He's playing some of the newer things by Sammy Nestico, which are fine arrangements. He's got a lot of good people like this trombone player, Dennis Wilson, who is really excellent. And, I'm not saying I don't enjoy the band, but there is a different feel that the Basie Band has. I won't say they've lost, they've just given up or made a transition into a different style, a much more sort of well-oiled-machine type style.

Sammy Nestico

AUTHOR'S NOTE: But what a powerhouse of a machine. With arrangements as the years went by by Neal Hefti, Frank Foster, Nat Pierce, Quincy Jones, and Sammy Nestico to mention just a few. The excitement endured and grew. Far and away the most prolific of the latter day arrangers for the Count Basie Band was Sammy Nestico.

SAMMY: I remember when I first started writing for Basie, a fellow in the band said, "Sammy, I heard Basie talkin' last night and he said, 'You know the trouble with these young people that are always writin' for me, they want to write like Basie. They should write like themselves and we'll play it like Basie!'" I thought that was pretty funny so I said, "I'll remember that. I'll write like, more or less, like me. I won't try to write like every Basie album that's ever been out. But if I can write sparse and clean and clear and keep it simple—Basie's a simple man."

Listen to the way he plays piano. He's sparse and he has radar in his heel. When he set the time going, that was it! I mean the time's established. I really learned just by listening to and seeing what this man does. I said, "You know what, keep it simple, keep it melodic." I listened to Hefti. Neal is a great melodist. Neal Nefti and Henry Mancini are just great melodists. And I said, "You know, what Hefti's doing? He's writing nice melodies and he's blockin' 'em off and he's lettin' his guys swing, and that's exactly how I arrived at that kind of writing."

Neal Hefti

AUTHOR'S NOTE: Neal Hefti is not only a fine arranger, trumpet player, and composer, but after he left Woody Herman with his wife, Frances Wayne, he tried to form a band of his own. But he couldn't get it together, the management and a record company at the same time, those two things needed for success. This interview was in 1982.

NEAL: If we could get a record contract I would get it myself, you know, like just wearing out shoe leather and talking to someone. It was a time when we didn't have any management and we didn't have a record company contract. So, it's just in two parts, it's like going to Las Vegas again and pulling the thing and you get bell-lemon-lemon, and it really doesn't make. . .even get bell-bell-orange and it doesn't mean anything unless you get bell-bell-bell, you know. So we could never get that three bells at the same time. We could get one of them and not the other and we had them in all the different slots in different times in our lives but we could never get the sequence to go.

FRED: You sure had it all working for you when you did some of those Basie things. My God, he doesn't play a concert without playing three or four of your tunes. *Lil' Darlin'* is.

NEAL: Well, *Lil' Darlin,'* that's a standard for the band.

FRED: Oh, it is **the** standard. . .

NEAL: Yeah, yeah.

FRED: . . .In the book now.

NEAL: Yeah. Well, I made it for **him**, you know.

FRED: Yeah, but you did it.

NEAL: Yeah, but wait a minute, wait a minute. But see, he has the three bells going. He had the good band, he had the good record contract, he had the good booking agent and he had the good book and he had the good soloists. So, that's bell-bell-bell-bell-bell. You know what I mean?

FRED: Yeah.

NEAL: He had very great management. Willard was a very great manager for him, you know. And, I say that Morris Levy was a very, very good influence on Basie because he had that record company that let Basie do anything he wanted.

FRED: Roulette.

NEAL: Roulette, and anytime Basie had a free week he could play in Birdland.

FRED: And Morris Levy owned Birdland.

NEAL: Fred, it seemed like he's played there for six, seven months a year. You know what that meant for a band to play in New York? Home! And every time you got a week off you'd go right back. After awhile they didn't even say, when the ads would come out in the New York papers, they'd say, "He's home again." It wouldn't say, "Count Basie and His Orchestra," it wouldn't say "Birdland." It'd say, "He's Home Again." You know, I mean, that's what a thing he had going in those three or four years and you couldn't build a band without that and you couldn't built a band without a record company.

Frank Foster

AUTHOR'S NOTE: Despite the elusive quality of his leadership, there could never have been a band called the Count Basie Band without Count Basie, or a band that sounded like the Count Basie band without Bill Basie. And when the Count died in 1984, the band was without a leader, without The Chief. Then Thad Jones was elected to take over. Appointed the leader of the band. And then following him in 1986, Frank Foster. Frank had long been established as one of the great soloists of the Basie band, off and on through the years since the mid 1950s and one of the key arrangers and composers for the band as well. So he was well equipped. Frank was interviewed in 1986.

FRANK: Well, there's been a certain alteration in style due to the different styles of writing of guys like Eric Dixon and Sammy Nestico. Sammy Nestico practically established the style of the band in the late 60s and all through the 70s.

FRED: And yet the basic style was set in about 1936 or '37 with Eddie Durham and Count Basie working together and shaping it. Later, arrangers made it more sophisticated and complicated, but they sure stuck pretty much to the original formula.

FRANK: That's right, all they have to do is take the old man's advice, "keep it simple and make it swing." So, Sammy followed that formula using his own personal taste and you have the basic band of the 70s. Now I'm going to do the same thing and you're going to hear the new Basie band of the 80s and 90s with the Frank Foster touch, as well as the touch of certain individuals in the band like Dennis Wilson and Dennis Mackrel. We got about four or five writers in the band now.

FRED: You're a heck of a lot more than a ghost band.

FRANK: Definitely.

FRED: Really, it's a band with a future and you're looking at it that way.

FRANK: I should think so.

FRED: But is Bill Basie missed greatly in terms of the cohesiveness of the band, or were the last few years kind of painful when he wasn't feeling all that well?

FRANK: Well, you see, he was so near total incapacitation, I'll say the effectiveness of the band was reduced. Of course this was no fault of Mr. Basie's, age just caught up with him. But The Chief is missed in a spiritual sense. Yet his presence is felt. See, right now the band has a new energy.

FRED: Sure does.

FRANK: And so, we're better able to project the tradition into the future.

FRED: Is the band really on the road an awful lot? Night after night after night?

FRANK: Certainly. Yep! I would say on the average of 40 weeks a year we'll be on the road.

FRED: All over the country and overseas?

FRANK: All over the country and overseas! Yeah!

Count Basie

FRED: It seems to me that there aren't that many musicians around today who are really willing to put up with that. How do you account for the fact that these guys do?

FRANK: Well, see this is not just a road band, this is the **Count Basie Orchestra** and in addition to the prestigious nature of it, it's the most explosive force in jazz! What can I tell ya'?

FRED: It sure is. You know when the Basie band was here, before you joined the band, a month or two ago in Santa Barbara, I stood there with my fingers tingling and I think my hair was standing on end.

FRANK: Well, my hair stands on end every time I stand in front of these guys and wave my arms at 'em!

FRANK WESS, ERNIE WILKINS and
MARSHALL ROYAL (Ray Avery photo)

3

STEVE ALLEN

I first interviewed Steve Allen more than thirty years ago when, as a reporter for one of the radio networks, I was assigned to do a feature on SANE. Citizens For a Sane Nuclear Policy had been put together largely by Norman Cousins. Many prominent show-business names were involved. None was more articulate, persuasive, or as dead serious as Steve Allen, the comedian. SANE's object was to stop above-ground nuclear testing. Thanks to Steve and the others involved it succeeded. I learned that Allen was one of those rare "thinking" entertainers who was also remarkably accessible: a ready hand for a good cause.

Over the years we've talked a number of times and I've come to realize that few have done so much for so many talented musicians, composers and singers. This is because of Allen's TV visibility and partly because he was and is fiercely independent, and, most of all, because of his unfailing good taste. You'll find a few of those names in what follows, but only a few because Steve is and has always been involved in many creative projects. It would take a series of heavy volumes to do a fair overview. Here are some statistics: Steve has written more than 4,000 songs. He has, at last count, written 34 published books, fiction

STEVE ALLEN at the keyboard, his favorite place.

and non-fiction, that cover everything from philosophy, the new *Steve Allen On The Bible, Religion And Morality*, to the suspense novel, *Murder On The Glitter Box* and *Murder in Manhattan*, featuring a leading character called Steve Allen!

Steve was the host of the original "Tonight Show" as well as his own prime-time "Steve Allen Show" and of many subsequent network strips and "specials." With his wife, actress and comedienne Jayne Meadows he created the PBS "Meeting of Minds" series and won an Emmy for his efforts. His radio career began on local stations in Phoenix and Des Moines, jumped to Los Angeles and Mutual-Don Lee, and then to a late night CBS stint that is remembered with reverence, especially by those of us who used to drive 100 miles to be there in person. As late as 1989 Steve was doing a daily, all ad-lib radio show on NBC! In movies, Allen is best remembered for his title role in "The Benny Goodman Story." A recent activity has been appearances with his M.D. son, Steve, Jr., in a series of discussions and forums on Good Humor and Good Health. It was right after such a session at Santa Barbara City College in 1989 that I posed this first question:

FRED: Are we in danger of losing our sense of humor in this nation today?

STEVE: I don't think so. Sometimes people assume that because times are difficult there therefore will be less humor. Oddly enough, or perhaps not oddly enough, if you really know the function of humor and laughter, there is more laughter in difficult times. Bob Hope is never so popular as when there's a war going on and if the average person just considers the subject matter of jokes, comedy is about tragedy. The raw material of almost all the jokes you've ever heard is very tragic experience and often tragic reality. But rather than spend all our time weeping about the woes of humankind, just as a sort of a vacation from that, as it were, we've somehow learned or been blessed with, as the case may be, the ability to laugh.

FRED: Interesting. I think that during the depression which was the most difficult period in my life, people were able to laugh and what's more, I think the most creative period in our history musically was then, certainly in the writing of songs.

STEVE: Yes, that was a true golden age. That's why it's so great that you do what you do about good music and concentrating on it.

FRED: At piano you were essentially self-taught?

STEVE: Well, I started out the right way with neighborhood lessons and school lessons, but it didn't work out at the first exposure. Immediately I discovered I was not a terribly good reader, but the gift for composition emerged and I began to write little songs. I didn't start to write songs on any serious or extended basis until I was about 13 or 14.

FRED: When you say write songs, what did you do about putting them down on paper?

STEVE: Well, to this day I don't. There is a method I have if I'm somewhere where I don't have the right kind of taping equipment. I write down the letters of the alphabet, a, b, c, d, so forth, and that, at least, is enough. While no one else could read that to play from, at least it's enough to give me a memory aid if I look at the piece of paper a week later. But that's a rare situation when I do that. For the most part, 99% of my songs, I just record them at a piano into a tape recorder and then when I get maybe 15 or 20 songs on a cassette I send that cassette to somebody who can't compose a note, but can put down on paper whatever he hears. So that's how it gets written down.

FRED: I interrupted you. You were in your early teens when you started to play?

STEVE: Well, anyway, I started, as I say, the right way. My first lessons were probably when I was seven or eight or nine years old, but we moved around a lot. I went to 18 schools in all, lived in quite a few cities except for one period of my life for about a year and a half. We did not have a piano in the home or apartment. If you don't have a piano to practice on lessons don't really mean that much. So I never really took up the piano seriously until I was 13 or 14 and that was the day when Eddie Duchin, as you'll recall, was a big national hero, piano player and band leader. And at first I tried to play like him. To this day every kid plays those Eddie Duchin introductions.

FRED: And then they do *Heart and Soul*.

STEVE: They do the first 16 bars of *Heart and Soul*. That won't take you through the bridge, but it'll take you the first 16 bars. So our gang too used to do that, three or four of us were interested in music and one of them would play the left hand, the Eddie Duchin part and somebody else would play either one finger or two fingers in octaves up above. And one day I literally figured out that if I could play the left hand part with my left hand and the right hand part with one finger, then I wouldn't need a friend to do that. So I just sat there and taught myself to play with one hand what I had already been playing with two hands, the bass part, and that's the point at which my piano playing as we now know it really got started. Then about two years later I eased into jazz and that helped too.

FRED: Strikes me that you and Neal Hefti have a lot in common in terms of how you conceptualize melody and also the titles you give your pieces. He told me once that he just thought they ought to be straight and to the point and describe in general what you were going to hear.

STEVE: Oddly enough, I never give the titles any thought, so whatever the result is, it's come out of the subconscious, I suppose. In some cases the titles have no meaning whatever; that's very common in my writing because I write such an enormous volume of music, far more than the world needs from me or from any ten composers, I suppose. I've written thousands of songs, as you may know. So the main reason I have to give them some title, even though there may be no thought to a given melody in the absence of a lyric, is so I can locate the stuff in the files because I don't remember a tune literally ten minutes after I write it.

FRED: What about a song called *Mister Moon*? That's a knock-out of a melody.

STEVE: Thank you. That one might have started with a little head start in your unconscious or subconscious because it was the original theme of the old Tonight Show. I originally took it out and put in a song called *This Could Be The Start of Something Big*. For another reason I'll tell you about it in a moment. But I noticed that jazz musicians picked up that *Mister Moon* thing very early. Ella used to sing it in some of her club appearances. She would just do it scat because she never did know the words. And I think Steve Lawrence once recorded it. Bud Shank and Bob Cooper did it as a jazz thing about 15 or 20 years ago and it does make a good big band arrangement. But you know, you said something quite insightful when you were kind enough to link me with Neal Hefti. Neal is one of my favorite composers. Most people think of him as an arranger, but he's written a lot of very fine tunes. And the thing I liked—well, two things strike me about Neal Hefti's arranging and composing because as you may know, many of his arrangements are his own compositions. That's a lot of originals. And he's also arranged some of my things over the years.

But the first thing that strikes me is that I think of all the arrangers who have ever arranged for the Basie band—this, at least was true for a good many years—whether it was the last six months, I'm not sure. He was "the blackest of them all" and as you know, he's white. He really got some very groovy, funky stuff going. It was typical Basie; many of those old Basie classics were Neal Hefti compositions that the band just played brilliantly. So he had the Basie style down perfectly which is why Count Basie did so many of Neal's things.

Second thing I like about Neal's composing and arranging is that he's highly melodic. There are some good big band arrangers who, unless they're working with a Gershwin melody or something, if they give you an original, you really don't whistle it. You know, it may swing or there may be some good voicings, but there's nothing there to whistle much. Whereas when Neal writes, there's a pretty melody. You can, as the old saying goes, sing it on the way out of the theater.

FRED: Well, you write pretty much as he does, really a 32-bar construction, don't you? It's a A-A-B-A sort of a . . .

STEVE: Well, a good part of my things are that. Probably more than any other one form, but I write a lot in the blues form and some extended 64-bar things. *This Could Be The Start of Something Big* is a very long song. I wrote the lyric to what is probably the longest popular song or jazz song in the world in musical modern history and that is *South Rampart Street Parade*. It consists—I haven't counted them—I think it's seven totally separate melodies. It's really a sort of a Dixieland symphony and it just builds from one phrase to the next rather than repeating the original eight or something of that sort.

FRED: Again, who recorded that?

STEVE: Well, it came, as you know, out of the old Bob Crosby band originally.

FRED: Bob Haggart, though . . .

STEVE: Well, there's four guys' names credited with the composition of the music: Bob Haggart, Ray Bauduc and I forget who the other two are. They probably were members of the band too. They first recorded it I think around 1937 or '8—the old Bobcats. And in '51 after I wrote the lyric, later then, when we did it on some TV show I asked Bob and Ray. I said, "Who wrote what?" Because I'm always curious if you see four or five guys names on any tune, who wrote what. It's not likely they each wrote 25%, you know. And the answer was something I never expected to hear. They said in effect, "You know, we don't really know. In fact, we're not sure that we made up any of this stuff because basically this tune consists of Dixieland cliches and licks that we remember hearing years ago. We just kind of collected them all together, you know, fixed them up a little bit, rewrote them a little bit, and sort of scotch taped it together." But I'm sure glad they did because it's one of the jazz classics.

FRED: Who did record the vocal version?

STEVE: Well, the first recording with my lyrics we started right at the top—Bing Crosby and the Andrews Sisters.

FRED: How do you view your singing?

STEVE: I think I'm in the category of people like a Fred Astaire, Johnny Mercer. I'm certainly not in the category of a Perry Como or a Frank Sinatra. But the critics are generally very kind to me. Also it depends pretty much on what I'm singing. I did something years ago where I put out two albums of jazz piano, one sort of ultra beyond Monk, you know, real meaningless changes and certain strange dissonances and hitting notes with my elbow and stuff. We wrote some scholarly liner notes on the album cover and took a picture of a lovely woman who was our housekeeper at the time, a black woman named Mary Sears. We put her picture on the cover with her hands on the piano in our living room and you know, the jazz critics liked it.

FRED: And they took it seriously?

STEVE: Yeah. When they thought I was a black woman they kind of liked my playing. I happen to play fair boogie-woogie, so we did the same thing again. In this case the album was titled, "The Discovery of Buck Hammer," and the liner notes alleged that Mr. Hammer had recorded only this one album. He was a boogie-woogie specialist and worked in a small town in Mississippi or Alabama or someplace. He had unfortunately died not long after making this album. He was a little strange personally, preferred obscurity, had no interest in fame or money, and that was the story. And the jazz critics loved that album too. So a lot has to do with the image people have of you.

In fact, I was performing just a couple of weeks ago at a great jazz club in Washington, D.C. called Charlie's Georgetown and I said one night after singing a few tunes and the audience was very kind to the singing—I said, "Well, I appreciate your nice applause." And I wasn't singing my tunes; I was singing *It Had To Be You* and some old songs. I said, "You know, it's an interesting thing that there are three talk show hosts who originally were professional vocalists. Do you know who they are? It's a trivia question." And, of course, people over 50 do know. It's Merv Griffin, Mike Douglas and myself. I used to make my living as a singer before there was television. So I said, "But it really doesn't matter how well Merv Griffin or I sing or how poorly, for that matter. If we sang like Caruso we would never really be imprinted on the public consciousness as singers because we're known as doing something else." I said, "Also, our physical appearance is not harmonious with the image of a sexy crooner voice." I said, "I look like I teach history at a small Catholic college in the Midwest someplace. I don't look like a singer. And Merv Griffin looks like he's in real estate. He doesn't look like a singer either." So that's, I think, what people very often respond to.

FRED: I didn't know you made your living as a singer. I remember you first from the Mutual-Don Lee daily show you did with Wendell Noble.

STEVE: Yeah, and on that Wendell did most of the singing. I would sing comedy numbers and Wendell did the straight things. He had a lovely sort of a more authentic baritone voice. He sang in church and so forth. But my singing was always of the pop genre, but I used to sing with the local bands in Des Moines and in Phoenix and I had my own singing show on the Arizona network in Phoenix before I came over to Los Angeles. Once in a while on my old late night radio shows in the 1940s I'd do some vocals. As a matter of fact, when a local radio man here named Paul Worth put together a radio tribute several months ago to Johnny Mercer, he was able to unearth the audio track of a vocal duet. It ran about eight minutes that Johnny and I did on one of my old shows back in the late '50s. I mention those two albums that people loved when they didn't know I was the player, because I think I'm going to put out a vocal album soon and call it "The Romantic Voice of George Krelm" or whatever and we'll see what reviews it gets because then nobody will know it's me and they'll either like the voice or they won't. I think it'll be an interesting experiment.

FRED: I want to talk about other singers in a moment, particularly those that you brought to national fame on the original Tonight Show, but first, back to the piano. Your favorite jazz pianist—who would that be?

STEVE: If God said, "You shalt listen to only one piano player for the rest of your life . . ." If I had to make that silly choice, I would choose Erroll Garner because he had really at least two separate styles and maybe even more than that. There was the Garner of the lacey, graceful ballads, the romantic, moody things which, strictly speaking, was not jazz except in some of its harmonics, and then there was the other player, the jazz player on the fast tunes, you know. And there, too, he played his own style. He had a unique percussive style. He didn't read music either; he was self-taught. I guess that's why he developed his own style. He never had the kind of chops that an Oscar Peterson does or Paul Smith or Art Tatum or whoever. But if anybody's good I love them. Dave McKenna is terrific, he's very individual. I was thinking the other day in my car that if Bach were alive and could play jazz piano he would play like Dave McKenna.

FRED: You were able to get a lot of jazz, a lot of good music, on the original Tonight Show. How did it ever reach NBC?

STEVE: Well, in the first form of it, it was just called the Steve Allen Show. It was a local show in New York and then at the end of the year Pat Weaver decided to put it on the full network. But I sometimes refer to what happened then when I quit the show, about two and a half years later, in some of my speeches about thinking and about general semantics. Traditionally, and going back into radio, let's say, if there was something called the Joe Dokes Show and Joe Dokes decided to move to Montana and stop his show, the show would go off. Nobody would ever have thought to get somebody else to star in the Jack Benny show because the name was the show. Well, for some reason or other NBC made that same kind of dumb mistake when I told them I didn't want to do the Tonight Show any more, because they had also put me on a prime time comedy show Sunday nights which paid about five times as much and had an enormous audience. So I took the better of the two deals—glad I did. But I always assumed that they were gonna have somebody else go on with the Tonight Show and I recommended Jack Parr or Ernie Kovaks. I said, "They could do that. They would do it a little differently than I did, but they could do it." And NBC was not interested in that, isn't that silly? They decided to put on a terrible program called America After Dark, one of the worst shows they ever did—anybody ever did. It was so terrible they took it off quickly and they really didn't want to put the Tonight Show back on but they had no third alternative at the moment, so while they were ad-libbing, trying to think of what else to do, they just put the Tonight Show back on and had Jack Parr and then, of course, they gradually realized that's what they should have kept all along.

FRED: Was the original show, the original Tonight Show, the outgrowth of the Steve Allen Show, more involved with music than the show is today?

STEVE: Oh yes, much more, and more involved with comedy too. Of course, Johnny Carson's a comedian, so he does a certain amount of it. In addition to his opening monologue he does a certain amount of sketches. But we did more. We did more craziness, more experimental things. I can never say the show was better, that's for other people to decide. And I would never even say, "I'm funnier than any other comedian." That's for other people to decide, too. But minute for minute, pound for pound, so-to-speak, we did more nonsense on the old show than has been done any time since then. Then, also, because I'm a musician with a particular interest in jazz, music too, was much more important during my three and a half years. The band in those days was just not used to coming in and out of commercials as they basically are ever since, or to accompanying an occasional singer. We had them on camera a lot, we had them do numbers.

FRED: Who led the band, Skitch?

STEVE: Skitch Henderson in those days. The original year was Bobby Byrne, the old trombone player and band leader. To this day I've never known why Bobby Byrne didn't continue. I was on vacation for about a week and when I got back somebody said, "Oh, by the way, Skitch Henderson is the leader now." And I said, "Oh, really? I didn't know that." And then they said, "It's time to go to rehearsal," and I never did get the story and still don't know how it happened. But anyway, Bobby used to be featured and people knew that Doc Severinsen was in the band and Yank Lawson was in the band and Lou McGarity and Bobby Rosengarden was the drummer and a lot of good players. Sweets Edison played in the band sometimes. So another factor was that we had all the jazz greats. I think the only one we never had was Charlie Parker. I don't know why that was—I would have loved to have him. But I don't remember that he was ever on the show, but I think practically every other one that we knew about was there.

FRED: And some great singers.

STEVE: Oh, yes. Well, we had not only all the good singers come on as guests, but we had our own regular family singers. Steve (Lawrence) and Eydie (Gorme) and Andy Williams are the three everyone remembers. The original singer was a young lady named Helene Dickson who sang very well, although a strange thing happened. We auditioned people, naturally. We were looking for basically beginners, not known. She was the best of those who auditioned, so we hired her. And she sang her three songs like on a Monday, on a Wednesday and a Friday, three songs she had auditioned with, and then the next week we said, "Well, now, tonight why don't you do *Stardust* or something?" And she said, "I don't know that." And we said, "Well, don't worry about it, what do you know?" And she said, "I just know those three songs." And I said, "Well, could you learn some more?" And she said, "Well, not for quite some time." Anyway, so they had to let her go.

   Then we got a singer named Pat Kirby who was marvelous and at a certain point we had Pat Marshall who's since been married to Larry Gelbert. She had come out of MGM. Bill Harbach, our producer, knew her from Hollywood, and she was quite good. So there were all good singers in those days.

FRED: This was really the first major engagement for Steve and Eydie together? Did they come on the show together? Were they married at the time?

STEVE: No, they didn't even know each other. They met on the show. I had hired Steve first. It was Steve Lawrence and Helene Dickson who were our two original vocalists. He had, just two or three nights before, I don't know whether he won it or was just on it—but anyway, one of those Arthur Godfrey talent scouts, amateur hour things and he was, I think about 17, and he had a white sailor suit and a white sailor hat. He wasn't in the Navy, this was just his costume, but I don't think he had much other wardrobes. So he showed up for our show in his sailor outfit and it looked cute and he sang very well. He still sings great. So he stayed with us and then it was quite a few months after that—several months, I think, that we added Eydie. I was recording for Coral Records at the time. I just happened to run into Eydie up at the offices at Coral and Decca one day. Bob said, "Oh, by the way, this is Eydie Gorme, she's a very good singer." And we just happened to be looking for somebody at that time so I said, "Why don't you come over to the theater sometime this week and do a couple of tunes for us?" So that's all there was to that and then she and Steve met.

FRED: And they're still at it today. I think the best recording of *This Could Be The Start of Something"* is theirs.

STEVE: Yeah, it still holds up. They did it recently on the Music Room Shows. It was a great arrangement and still swings.

FRED: Andy Williams was with the Williams Brothers up until the point he came on your show?

STEVE: Yeah, he had been with the Williams Brothers and Kay Thompson and hadn't done that much alone. Of all the people I've worked with over the years, about the only one who has since become a big star and whose success surprised me a little bit, because I thought he was too good to be big, was Andy. I loved his singing right from the start. How can you not like him? He's a very nice fellow and he has a lovely sound. He makes a pretty noise with his mouth and he had very good taste. He was always singing Porter or Rogers and Hart, Jerome Kern or something. I never heard him sing a dumb song.

At one point or two he had to record a few dumb ones because all singers have had to do that. But when it was up to our show and his own taste, he sang nothing but the best. But this was at a time in the '50s when American music quality-wise was beginning a long slide which I'm afraid continues to the present day. We had come out of the 30 years of golden age period '20s, '30s and '40s of Berlin and Kern and Romberg and Victor Herbert and all these glorious writers—Gershwin and Johnny Mercer and, well, you know the names—Jimmy Van Heusen. These men were giants. And then suddenly—with a few good exceptions, of course—there were still some show tunes, *My Fair Lady* and other marvelous things did happen. But basically it was suddenly bobby sox music and *Beach Blanket Bingo* and black leather jacket music and garbage music. So in that context I thought, "Andy's got too much class to ever be a hit today." So I was very gratified to be wrong about that.

FRED: Of course, as a singer, a pianist, a composer, a comedian yourself, you got a chance to show off your material a lot.

STEVE: I can get into a nightclub or a concert or something, whether they hire me as a singer or a comedian, it doesn't matter, or a composer. I do symphony dates where I don't do any comedy and I just play my songs on the piano. I have that slight advantage, so I can get exposure for my songs and most people have no judgment, even most professional singers have the judgment of a dummy if they just hear a song with the composer or the lyricist doing it with one piano. I went through that with a million of my songs. In fact, it happened with two of my songs which turned out standards. I knew they were good. I'd written them for the same musical. One song was *This Could Be The Start of Something Big* and the other was *Impossible*.

FRED: Which musical?

STEVE: The musical was called *The Bachelor*. It was on NBC television. It was one of those big spectaculars as they used to call it. And it was a nice show. I just wrote the songs, I didn't write the rest of the show. So I began to show other singers those songs too and particularly these two. And this is what happened in every case. About both songs people would say, "Those are very good songs; they're very New Yorky kind of show tunes. What do you have that's more popular style, you know, more Hit Parade style?" I used to grit my teeth, but I heard it so many times, so I finally stopped arguing, stopped showing people the tunes. I threw out *Mister Moon* which was my old theme and put in *This Could Be The Start of Something Big*, and I threw out my old *Good Night* theme, you know, like a good night song and put in *Impossible* and in two months the result was exactly as I'd predicted.

When people heard them every night and every week, suddenly they knew them and loved them. So now the singers were coming to me saying, "What is that great song that you play when you go off every night? Boy, is that pretty." And I would say, "Hey, jerk, I showed it to you eight months ago and you didn't pick up on it." You know. But anyway, at that point, they became immediate standards. There are over 100 recordings of *This Could Be The Start* and there've been about 35 recordings of *Impossible*.

FRED: Let me say my favorite is the one by the Singers Unlimited.

STEVE: Boy, you have good taste. Originally done, as you know, by the Hi-Lo's with a Frank Comstock arrangement. I was so thrilled by that arrangement that I wrote—somehow I ended up writing the liner notes for the album. I was so impressed by the whole album, because I always loved the Hi-Lo's, that I wrote it in the form of poetry rather than just prose.

FRED: In TV you did a daily show for a while. Mostly it seems to me you were sitting at the piano when you did the show, weren't you? Or it was right next to you? What was that—a thing you did for Westinghouse or one of those people?

STEVE: Whenever I've done a talk-show formula I've always used the piano to open with. In fact, to this day, if I ever sit in for Johnny or Merv or any other talk-show host, for that matter, on their day off, I open at the piano in center stage and do my first five or ten minutes there either playing or horsing around or doing comedy. It's just a simple, obvious place for me to be as it is for Victor Borge or Liberace or any other player. So I don't know what show it is you might have seen. On most of them we also had a talk-show host desk over at the other side of the stage, but the piano was always dominant.

FRED: I just remember the set was very intimate indeed and there was always music close by and so were the musicians who played with you.

STEVE: Well, one show that you might be thinking of, come to think of it, on that we did not have the typical talk-show host desk, was the very first regular series I ever did on television on a network. That was for CBS in 1951 and '52. It started every night at—it was either 7:00 or 7:30. I think it was from 7:00 to 7:30—30 minutes, and I would use the piano as my place to work from.

FRED: A hundred percent live, I'm sure.

STEVE: Oh, yeah, in those days. I used to scream, "Stop tape," but nobody would know what I meant. They hadn't invented tape yet. Anyway, it was indeed live and it was kindly received, but that may have been the one where you saw me at a piano every day.

FRED: Seems to me you must be at the typewriter every day, looking at the volume of fiction and non-fiction you turn out— book after book. Let's talk about a few of them, for example . .

STEVE: Well, I have one that's a history of talk-shows, another one called "How To Think." It's about the collapse of intelligence in the American population and what might be done about it.

FRED: What can be done about it, Steve? In a few words, as they say in the Lehrer/MacNeil Show. What can be done about that?

STEVE: Well, oddly enough, this particular social problem has a fairly simple solution. I emphasize fairly because there are complexities. But most of the big problems are so incredibly complex that the solution, by no means, immediately presents itself. The nuclear weapons dilemma, for example. God, the best minds of our time for the last 30 years have wrestled with that one and the only people who have at least a consistent approach are the Pacifists and, of course, the world will never pay attention to them so, so much for that. But as regards what we can do to prevent the American people from getting dumber, I've been recommending for about 25 years the addition of a fourth "R" to the traditional reading, writing and arithmetic. The fourth "R" is reasoning. I think we are going to have to start teaching people how to reason, how to think, at the kindergarten or first grade level. The only instruction they get in it now is likely to be at the university level and those get it who need it least. They're already interested in that so they soak up a little more. But most people reason very poorly indeed, and that has become a danger to our society. It would certainly horrify the Jeffersonians who had something else in mind—the other founding fathers.

FRED: Steve, you're at it, obviously, from the moment you wake up until you go to sleep, and for all I know, while you're sleeping. What do you do when you want to relax and get away from just everything?

STEVE: Well, Fred, I'm very fortunate. I practically never reach that point. Most people do one thing for a living and in some cases they're under terrible pressure — maybe economic pressures or personal pressures or the work may be boring. You know, the kind of thing that Charles Chaplin had in mind when he made *Modern Times*. You know, a guy turning two screws and a bolt on a factory line all day long. If you did that for a living you would really have to get away and go fishing or whatever. But in my case, all my work is pleasant. I was doing all these things for fun before it ever occurred to me I could make a living at it. And I am rarely frustrated in my professional life. I should not say that I never am, because we live in a vale of tears. But my life, really, has much more laughter and reward to it than most people's. So I never get that feeling of being totally wiped out. And upon occasion if it happens for physical reasons, like not enough sleep for three nights in a row, I just take a 14 hour vacation in bed and then jump into the pool and have a little orange juice and I'm as good as ever.

FRED: You must be very fortunate in your choice of spouses because obviously your wife has got to live the same life, pretty much.

STEVE: Well, I am fortunate, of course, in my choice of wives, but Jayne and I live lives that are partly separate and partly a matter of togetherness. We obviously live in the same house, but she has a career of her own. She doesn't have to bring me breakfast in bed every morning, although upon rare occasions, she does, now that I think of it. But I don't expect that she will be my servant, only my wife, you know. And I'm quite self-sufficient in the kitchen. I sometimes don't even bother our housekeeper. I'll just go in the room and make lunch for myself. My physical needs are few. I'm very easily pleased about food, clothing, hotel rooms, whatever. And so Jayne and I really don't get in each other's way. We like to work together. Sometimes when I do my comedy concerts she works in the show, which I much prefer. And if she's doing a show—she is this week—I'll do some rehearsing with her, I'll play director, I'll take her through a scene and make some instructive comments about it and she'll do the same for me if I'm in a film or a TV show that she's not working on. So we seem to have struck a happy balance as regards those factors.

FRED: One project on which you worked together was called, "The Meeting of Minds," PBS series—an extraordinary one on historical figures.

STEVE: Suddenly there's a renewed wave of interest in that, by the way. I'm not sure why that is. I think it has something to do with the revolution in cable and computer and cassette and video tape recorders and all that. Within the last few weeks four separate distribution companies have approached us—all from different points of the compass—asking to distribute those 24 shows.

STEVE: You own the show?

FRED: I co-own them with KCET, the PBS television station with whom they were produced, so we don't have time right now—I don't have time to turn out any more of those shows, although I might at some future point. But they have, I discovered, millions of fans around the country and other parts of the world too. It's quite popular in Latin America. It's been seen in Japan. I recently got the cassette with the Spanish language track on it. It looked funny to see myself speaking Spanish. I think of all the things I've done, it's the only thing that will ever be remembered after I'm gone. A thousand years from now I think people will still be watching those cassettes. They won't know who the tall guy with the glasses is, but they'll still know who Aristotle was. They'll know who Socrates was and so forth.

FRED: Steve, *The Benny Goodman Story*, this I think happened while you were still working out of New York with television. Were you going back and forth?

STEVE: Yeah, I did the Tonight Show at the same time, Fred, and I do mean at the same time. We got permission from the network to do it here in Los Angeles, of course, and we were on the air live at the time, so we were put up at the Ambassador Hotel. I'd be on the air live from 11:30 to 1:00 in the morning, New York time, then we'd go to bed, have to get up about 4:00, be taken to Universal, work all day, rushed in the limousine, totally wiped out, back to do the Tonight Show, which I hardly remember now because I was in a daze for the nine weeks or whatever that we did that. But that's how it worked out. But it was great fun working with Gene Krupa and Teddy Wilson and . . .

FRED: Did you play clarinet at all?

STEVE: The only scene in the movie where you hear me actually playing is the scene where Benny is nine years old and playing the scales on his first instrument because Benny himself pre-recorded all those big band numbers, but he could not make the sound a beginner makes; he was not able to. But I was learning the instrument at that time, so that was my natural tone. So it's me you hear playing the scale.

FRED: But obviously you knew the fingering or learned the fingering.

STEVE: Yeah, I thought I could just do with, you know, cute footwork and body moves or something, but I soon realized I had to learn the instruments so that my fingers would be on the right holes at the right time.

FRED: And did you study Benny in person and watch him considerably?

STEVE: Not much. I studied with Sol Yaged, who is a Benny Goodman freak, as you know, and knows all Benny's solos and his mannerisms. Benny himself wasn't available. Benny was really out of town by the time I got to the job. Benny was off on his own planet anyway, as you know. So he wasn't around much.

FRED: We started this off talking about good health and its relation to good humor and then we've gone on to one triumph after another for you, Steve. But I know there were plenty of hard times in-between and you've recently undergone a bout of serious illness which you conquered well and you're moving on to new things. Looking back, can you sort of grin and bear it about the whole thing? Is there laughter to go with the sad moments?

STEVE: Yeah, I look back on almost everything and look forward to almost everything with a smile and a laugh. I'm very fortunate in that way. I was playing around, as I do every few days, with one of my grandchildren. His name is Bradley. He's my son Bill's little boy. He's three years old, and he clearly has inherited—now it sounds weird to say that there are genes that have something to do with wit and funniness and silliness—but I'm coming to think that is the case. I love all my grandchildren equally; I have six, but they're not all equally funny any more than they're equally tall or equally heavy or equally anything else. And he is just a naturally funny kid. He's also hyper and a bit of a scamp and gets himself into certain kinds of little innocent difficulties. And I said to Bill the other day when he was acting naughty, but he was still laughing. I said, "You know, laughter will be Bradley's salvation." And Bill said, "I know what you mean." He reminded me of my mother in that way. She had in many regards an utterly tragic life, but her wit kept her from going crazy.

FRED: Well, you're in the business of making life worthwhile, both with music and with humor.

STEVE: Yeah, it's an important service. I don't think any of us should be conceited about it because we didn't give ourselves those gifts and most of us didn't even work very hard to be able to do that. It's like being tall; either you're tall or you're not or you're Armenian or not. It's just whatever you are, you are.

Steve Allen

STEVE ALLEN, right with pianist TEDDY WILSON, on the set of "The Benny Goodman Story." (Ray Avery Jazz Archives)

64

4

TEDDY WILSON

In jazz, the piano has to be first among instruments. It stands alone and works well in any size combo. In a big band the piano is the pivotal source of rhythm and traditionally serves to modulate to a singer's key, provide the introductory bars to an arrangement and, of course, take solo spots. Practically every musician started on piano. There was a time when half the population of any civilized country could play it and most homes had at least an upright. Of all the pioneers who set the styles and expanded the limits of the keyboard, three remain paramount to this day. They are Earl Hines, Art Tatum and Teddy Wilson. Teddy, as you will see, learned from the other two and studied with many great teachers, both in jazz and classical traditions. His playing was often torrid, at incredible tempos, but his manner was never less than gentle and elegant and so were his conceptions of style and improvisation. "Chamber Jazz" clearly originated with the Benny Goodman Trio and Wilson's finesse was the essence of its performances.

Teddy was helped by jazz champion John Hammond, who put all his wealth and considerable energies to work in a lifetime of promoting jazz artists, mostly black (Goodman being one exception). He saw that they recorded often and well. My earliest thrills in recorded jazz were listening to the still fabulous all-star recordings Teddy made for Brunswick in the mid-to-late 30s, promoted by Hammond. When I was able to bring Teddy to my town of Ojai, California, in 1981, to play in the Festivals Bowl with Benny Carter, Red Norvo and other greats, I must admit that it was the opinion of my co-producing partner, Lynford Stewart, and myself that after thirteen years of our JAZZ AT OJAI concerts, we had reached the pinnacle.

Afterwards, as was the custom following all the jazz concerts, the musicians and others came to my home to a party hosted by my wife, Gita. It was said by many, that even more than the pay, this informal get-together of the musicians and some of their friends, whom they may not have seen for years, brought some of the very greatest to Ojai. Teddy and I talked on tape for an hour or more. He died about five years later but his presence continues to be felt and heard every time you listen to almost **any** good or great pianist. Look for his classic records with Billie Holiday, with the Benny Goodman Trios, Quartets, Sextets and Septets and under his own name. As this is being written, many are being reissued on CDs. They are to be treasured.

FRED: Teddy, I want to talk particularly about the Brunswick Record days, if you don't mind, because I find them very interesting, but first: a couple of questions for you. You studied a lot of instruments, didn't you? Not just piano?

TEDDY: I played violin and oboe and some E-flat clarinet in the marching band in school—in high school.

FRED: Which was where?

TEDDY: Tuskegee Institute, Alabama.

FRED: Your father was a teacher, there?

TEDDY: He was head of the English Department at Tuskegee. My mother taught in elementary grades.

FRED: Did he want you to go into a musical career, or . . .

TEDDY: No, I got into this career after he died. He died quite young. He was only 50. I got the jazz fever after that, about age 14.

FRED: How did you get bitten?

TEDDY: Recordings. The Louis Armstrong recordings, King Oliver's recordings of those days, and especially after Earl Hines joined the Hot Five. I got to hear the *West End Blues*, pieces like that. We were also able to get Fats Waller recording solos. *A Handful of Keys*, I had that. And around the school there, there were some students who were excellent players. There was a guy named Melvin Smalls, who you never hear of, who played at many of the teacher's house parties. We had a wonderful teacher: pianist at the school. They didn't have sound movies in those days. The silent movies they'd show in the chapel. This man was from the City and he taught English Literature in the senior and junior classes of high school. He would play the piano at all the movies. He was a wonderful player. But these people played as a hobby like this Melvin Smalls., My favorite around there was a man who worked in the drug store. He was on the cash register selling cigarettes and candy. He wasn't a pharmacist. His name was John Lovette. This tenth bass that I use . . . he had this thing perfected in those days, that's the late 20s. That's where I learned it from. I was in John Lovette's home many times and John was a collector of records. I heard recordings of Duke Ellington playing piano solos and all the early Ellington records.

FRED: This was the late 20s?

TEDDY: Yeah. About 1928.

FRED: Every piano player I talk to today, Mel Powell, most recently, says, "Teddy's my man: Teddy and Earl," so I do want to know who influenced you.

TEDDY: Well Earl, I'd say, and Fats and then, shortly after, Art Tatum. Art was not on records as early as they were, but I was able to be around Art personally before either one of us ever made a record.

FRED: This was where, Detroit?

TEDDY: Toledo.

FRED: Did you do some radio shows together, the two pianos?

TEDDY: No, no, never did that, no. He was on the radio. As a matter of fact what happened is, he quit the job with the Milton Senior Band. Milton Senior was a clarinet player in Toledo, Ohio, and he had previously been third alto with McKinney's Cotton Pickers and left McKinney's Cotton Pickers to go home, (he had a young wife in those days) to live in Toledo. He had this job at a little club called Chateau La France and Art Tatum was playing piano with him. Then Art got a job at WSPD, still got the same call letters, to play half-hour piano solos five days a week at 5:00 in the afternoon. He left the night club job to do the radio and Milton Senior brought me in to replace Art in his little band at the Chateau La France. I was there for months and months. Oh, we'd get together most every night and he showed me a lot of things on the piano.

FRED: Still one of a kind.

TEDDY: Nobody like him. He's just the nearest to what we could call "a phenomenon" in almost any activity. Art, to me, was like a person who could pick up a baseball bat and he'd hit a home run every time. He could pick up a golf club and hit a hole-in-one every time. It was the most unusual ability in any human that I've ever seen—this exceptional, unexplainable skill and affinity he had with the keyboard.

FRED: Was he classically trained?

TEDDY: I think so. I think—I know he could read Braille and he went to a school for the blind in Columbus, Ohio.

FRED: He was partially blind all his life?

TEDDY: He played piano as a blind player—only by ear and touch.

FRED: How did you happen to wind up with Benny Carter?

TEDDY: John Hammond was largely responsible for that. John Hammond heard me after I had moved to Chicago. I made that my headquarters and was playing with the Eddie Moore band at the Grand Terrace when Earl Hines would go on the road. Earl Hines was one of the biggest stars of jazz in those days in broadcasting. His midnight broadcasts were on every night on NBC from the Grand Terrace. And so, when he'd go on the road, they'd hire this Eddie Moore band and I would play the piano. They would feature me because I could play Earl Hines style. A lot of people didn't know the difference. And so John Hammond was able to hear me on the radio because we'd come on the air at midnight. That would be 1:00 New York time and, in those days, there was no all-night radio. The New York stations went off at midnight.

So John Hammond called me to Benny Carter's attention and Benny came out to Chicago with a friend of his named George Rich. The two of them came out in this beautiful blue Cadillac. I'll never forget it. I was playing with Jimmie Noone at the time and Benny Carter offered me the job with his band back in New York. He also liked the trombone player, Keg Johnson, who was in Chicago (Bud Johnson's older brother). He brought me and Keg to join his band in New York where he was playing at the Harlem Club, which was owned by this man George Rich.

FRED: I remember a record, *I Never Knew*.

TEDDY: That's the earliest recording. First week, I think, that we were in New York we did these dates. John Hammond arranged those dates, I think, and they called them "The Chocolate Dandies." Max Kaminsky was on 'em, Floyd O'Brien, trombone, and he had, let's see, I think Sid Catlett did some of the drumming, maybe Cozy Cole. Chu Berry did some tenor 'cause Benny Carter was the leader in those days.

FRED: Those were good, good, great records. Weren't you with Willie Bryant somewhere along the line?

TEDDY: After Benny Carter gave up being a band leader, there for a while, I joined Willie Bryant. Benny also went with Willie and became his Musical Director, took over the band. It became like a musical Benny Carter band and it was a tremendous improvement for Willie Bryant's band. Willie was a great entertainer but not a musician. In those days you know, everybody had a "front man" for a band and, of course, Cab Calloway had been tremendously successful so Willie was sort of on the road to becoming another personality like Cab.

FRED: Playing places like the "Apollo," for instance?

TEDDY: Oh, everywhere, and radio. There was a circuit of theaters and one-night stands on the road. We'd do quite a few one-night stands. Savoy Ballroom would be our home base, owned by men named Moe Gale and Charlie Buchanan. And Chick Webb's band was in there. Part of that time, Teddy Hill's band . . .

FRED: Jimmy Lunceford . . .

TEDDY: Jimmy was more of a Cotton Club attraction. He went in the Cotton Club, along with Duke and Cab Calloway and a band called the Mills Blue Rhythm Band under a man named Baron Lee. But the Savoy bands would be Lucky Millinder, Teddy Hill, Chick Webb, Willie Bryant and smaller groups like the Savoy Sultans. But they would broadcast, too. Radio was the thing in those days, rather than records, so they would all broadcast and then after you'd get publicity going to the radio public, you'd go out and do a road tour—one-night stands.

FRED: Well, Willie's band was an all-star band in many ways. Wasn't Chu Berry in the band and Coleman Hawkins?

TEDDY: No, no. Benny Carter was the only star and he sort of ran the band musically, arranged for it and rehearsed it.

FRED: You did some arrangements, too?

TEDDY: I did a few, yeah. The band with the names in it was Teddy Hill's band. Roy Eldridge was with Teddy and, I think Dizzy Gillespie was with Teddy Hill at one time in the early days. Of course Cab had. . .all these fellows worked with him—Ben Webster, Hilton Jefferson.

70

FRED: The story about how the Goodman Trio began, is that literal that it began in Mildred Bailey's home?

TEDDY: Yes, at a house party at Mildred and Red's home. Mildred Bailey and Red Norvo, Forest Hills, Long Island.

FRED: And you were just fooling around . . .

TEDDY: Yeah, the party was going . . . everyone would get up and play. Benny had his clarinet there—we got in this jam session. John Hammond is the one who really got the Trio started, actually, because he set up a recording session and he wanted it like he'd heard it in Mildred and Red's living room without the bass because there was no bass there that night. So he hired Gene Krupa to do the drums and we came to the Victor studio and we made our first Trio recording.

FRED: What were the first sides, you remember?

TEDDY: They would be *Body and Soul* and *After You're Gone, Who*, and,I think, *Someday, Sweetheart* were the four tunes on that date.

FRED: When did the Quartet come into existence?

TEDDY: The Quartet came later, after Benny became a band leader. He brought me in around 1936 at Easter when he was doing the concerts Sunday afternoons at the Congress Hotel in Chicago. He put a jazz concert on every Sunday afternoon and brought me out from New York to be a guest on one of those things. At the time I was the intermission piano player at the Famous Door. Bunny Berigan used to play there with his Quartet—Wingy Manone, Louis Prima and those people. Benny asked me just to stay on. So I got a release from the Famous Door to quit without notice and they agreed to do it. I stayed right on with Benny as a regular traveling member of the group. It continued for three years for me. And then soon after that, on our next trip to Los Angeles, Benny heard Lionel Hampton. Lionel was working at a little club on Main Street. He brought Lionel into the Trio and made a Quartet.

FRED: You made some records on the Coast, in Hollywood, actually.

TEDDY: Let me see. The first time? The first Quartet records might have been made in California. I believe so.

FRED: My favorite of that whole batch is *Pick A Rib*. That was two sides and there's a little riff that was used to get into that thing which I think Benny also used on a couple of other sides, on *Bei Mir Bist Du Schoen* and, let's see, *Opus One-Half*. You remember all those records?

TEDDY: No, not too clearly. We used to do a lot of those little riffs. Lionel used to think up a lot of those little original tunes we used to do. Some ideas were mine, some were Benny's, a great many of them were Lionel's. We'd have long rehearsals, sometimes days of rehearsals to put those little arrangements together 'cause nothin' was written. We would throw out ideas and Benny would sort of choose the ones and fit the little arrangements so it would be a composite of all our ideas in the finished product. And we would just rehearse 'till we got 'em perfect, too!

FRED: They were perfect gems. Stand that way today.

TEDDY: Performance was just about as good as we could get it.

FRED: How did the Brunswick sessions, later re-issued on Columbia, come about? Was that John Hammond?

TEDDY: John Hammond again. He interested Brunswick in a series of all-star musicians and he was crazy about Billie Holiday. She was his favorite singer. I was never a Billie Holiday fan myself. But he introduced me to Billie soon after I got to New York. I liked the other singer in the club, a girl named Beverly White. They used to call her "Baby" White. And I liked her singing much better than Billie's, but he only liked Billie because John's tastes were very, very narrow. He liked Bessie Smith. The only women singers he liked were Bessie Smith, Mildred Bailey and Billie Holiday in those days.

FRED: You used Nan Wynn on some tracks. She was a good singer!

TEDDY: Nan was a lovely singer. She was more my style of singer than Billie Holiday. The singer who was with my big band, Jean Eldridge, was really my kind of singer and Beverly White, the other one I told you about, but Beverly never got a break. She sang a little while with Claude Hopkins' band but never got any significant recordings.

FRED: Was the idea to cover pop tunes for the so-called "race" market at that time?

TEDDY: I don't know what Brunswick was thinking of when they took us on. What we actually did bring was an "all-star" thing. There's no way in the world the public could see these people in person. Because, on those dates you'd have . . . the first date we had Benny Goodman next to Ben Webster and Roy Eldridge on trumpet and John Kirby bass, Cozy Cole on drums. On our other dates we had Johnny Hodges sittin' next to Buck Clayton. Harry Carney and Harry James and Gene Krupa were there too. These were like a . . . there was nothin' like 'em! 'Cause there was no public appearance where it was financially possible to have these men. They had the pick of Basie's band, of Ellington's band, of Chick Webb's band—these fellows I'd get together. And the only way you could hear them was on these records! The first time Johnny Hodges ever recorded away from Duke Ellington's band was on those all-star dates that we had. The whole thing was a very unique idea and I don't know whether Brunswick was thinking about "race" or anything, but musically there was nothing like it. The nearest thing in the past would have been when you get the collaboration of, say when you get a record with Frank Trumbauer, Bix Beiderbeck, Eddie Lang, Joe Venuti: those all-star things . . .

FRED: And later Lionel Hampton did it . . .

TEDDY: Lionel did it with RCA. Of course, Armstrong was generally the star of all of his. The nearest to me that he had of an all-star thing was when he teamed-up with Earl Hines. He had a man of his own stature and calibre.

FRED: You played with Louis, didn't you? I always thought those big bands of his weren't too good.

TEDDY: They weren't, no. Nothing special. The managers were only concerned with presenting Louis Armstrong as a personality and not interested in any musical group at all, just a background, any old background.

FRED: Now back to the Brunswick dates. Were these generally done early morning?

TEDDY: No, it would be various times of the day, according to when we could get everybody together 'cause lot of times musicians would be on the road.

FRED: Would you sketch-out some sort of . . .?

TEDDY: Yeah, I did most of the sketching of the little so-called arrangements. They were not really arrangements. They were just little sketches to . . . that gave just something to feature the soloists—the singer and the horn players and myself. Maybe what was written would be an introduction or a simple harmony behind the soloist. We might sometimes write out a little ending.

FRED: Who picked the tunes for the sessions?

TEDDY: I always picked them. We would put in some standards of that day and some brand new tunes. I was given a stack of new music by Jack Higgins who was head of this department . . . the direct official that I'd deal with at Brunswick Records there. Each month, he'd get a stack of music from all the publishers, all the new music that was published. He'd give me the stack to go through and pick out. We tried to do two or maybe three new tunes and then we'd put one or two standards in the dates, too. 'Cause there was not singing on all four songs, we'd do four songs on the date. But generally on two or maybe three songs, there'd be vocals on. We would always have an instrumental in there with no singing.

FRED: Billie was pretty young when she did the first things with you, wasn't she? A teen-ager?

TEDDY: I would think so. I didn't know her age. I never asked anybody her age. I'm not of that school of curiosity of people's age like so many people are, you know. So I never asked her. I would suspect a teen-ager.

FRED: Some of those sides of tunes that would have meant nothing otherwise came out pretty well. Oh, uh, *What A Little Moonlight Will Do*, for example . . .

TEDDY: That is still being played by disc jockeys in different places and by jazz fans. That was the first date. That was done about 1935.

FRED: Didn't it have a lot to do with the tempo?

TEDDY: It was an up-tempo tune. Well, almost every jazz singer in the world today, not only in America but in foreign countries, sings *What A Little Moonlight Will Do*. That one we made the first recording of. Another one we made the first recording of that all the singers do is *Easy Living*. We did the first record of *You Go To My Head*. Nan Wynn sang that one. Billie Holiday sang *Easy Living*.

FRED: *Why Was I Born* was . . .

TEDDY: Oh, that was an old tune. That was an old standard that had been done . . . that had been sung by a wonderful singer named Mae Alix in Chicago. A lot of people don't know who Mae Alix was. I've seen Mae Alix in night clubs reduce a whole audience to tears singing *More Than You Know*. It was just some of the most beautiful singing that was never publicized or ever recorded.

FRED: You think of Helen Morgan, at least I do, in terms of the old treatment of *Why Was I Born*. She did it in the show: "Showboat" and she used to do it later sitting on a white piano.

TEDDY: I remember she was famous for that piano. Those singers of that period I don't recall too much except there was one that I really liked on her recordings: Ruth Etting. I liked her singing, on records. And, of course, the best of 'em all was Ethel Waters. Ethel Waters, in the late 20s, was combining lyric and melodic lines like Frank Sinatra came to doing in the 40s. Ethel Waters was doing that in the 20s!

FRED: John Hammond saw that those were reissued.

TEDDY: Yeah?

FRED: Yeah . . . there's a whole double-pocket album.

TEDDY: Those ballads that she did . . . things like *You're Mine*. . . singers today don't even know about those songs.

FRED: What instrumentals from among the group you did for Brunswick stand out in your mind today as ones you enjoyed doing perhaps more than others?

TEDDY: Oh, no particular one. I don't have any one favorite. The way we, the way I approach music, we did those records. . . We would stay with those things until we got 'em right and then we would move on to the next, so they are all good. There's no one great big hit. They were 100% good or else we kept repeating! Get through with a record, ask Johnny Hodges, "You satisfied with your solo?" Buck Clayton, "Are you satisfied with your solo?" And when everybody is satisfied, well, we'd go to the next tune. So they're ALL good. There's no medium or excellent, they're ALL good. Every one. 'Cause that's the way we made 'em. And they're the best musicians in the world. At that time. The best in the world were on those dates and I just didn't feel that Billie Holiday was of the stature of these musicians as a singer. But Billie was a stylist and, too, Billie had a lovely sense of rhythm, and so it does sound appropriate. But I think . . . on a par with those musicians I would have preferred Ella, Ella Fitzgerald, in those days.

FRED: Well, you did a few sides with Ella.

TEDDY: Yeah. I think Ella was singing in a class with Benny Goodman's clarinet or Lester Young's playing the sax or Ben Webster and those kind of people.

TEDDY WILSON at a Jass at Ojai concert, August 1981. (Ray Avery photo)

FRED: You had a big band yourself, for a while. This was when?

TEDDY: That was about 1939.

FRED: And Ben Webster was in the band?

TEDDY: He was in the band.

FRED: Tell me about the band . . . was it just too tough to make that kind of a payroll?

TEDDY: Yeah, I didn't get cooperation from the booking office. MCA was the booking office and used the band as a football. And they were selling me cheap to keep promoters in their pockets with other bands they were pushin' because they weren't pushin' my band at all. They sold me on cheap jobs and just made it impossible to keep that group together. The band was hand-picked and, of course, Ben got an offer to go with Duke and I couldn't blame him for doing it. I couldn't compete with paying that. Harold Baker, one of my trumpet players later went with Duke, and Karl George went with Stan Kenton. J. C. Heard was on the drums. Al Casey went with Cab Calloway, J. C. went with Cab and things like that.

The band just fell apart economically because it wound up with a long-term engagement at the Golden Gate Ballroom in Harlem where the guys made, I think, about $38.00 a week or something like that and I was making about a hundred. I was having to support our arranger, Buster Harding, out of mine. It was just struggling unnecessarily because of no cooperation . . . and our records were not pushed. Even until this day, Columbia has never reissued the big band records of mine. They've reissued practically every record I've ever made with those small groups and some that were not too good, but none of my big band records. I have two copies of my big band, but they're bootlegged by two bootleg outfits, and they're selling all over the world. But Columbia never believed in 'em. I don't think John Hammond ever believed in that big band. Of course, John wasn't too fond of any big band except Basie. He loved Basie, but the written arrangements he didn't like except for those done by Fletcher Henderson that Goodman had. He didn't think you could put jazz on paper. Most of Goodman's arrangers I thought were marvelous: Eddie Sauter, Jimmy Mundy and some of the stuff Mel Powell did. I guess he was so young in those days, but you listen to those things now. . . he sounds like a man who had been writing arrangements for twenty years!

FRED: Mel, you know, is Dean Emeritus of Cal-Arts and it's hard to get him to play jazz any more. But he must be a direct descendant from you, Teddy. He sure credits you as his Number One influence! You went back with Goodman in what, about '45?

TEDDY: For the Seven Lively Arts show, yeah. He had Red Norvo on vibes, Morey Feld on the drums, and Sid Weiss on the bass. That was very nice. And then, after the show, Benny organized a big band again and he augmented our quintet to a sextet, only this time Slam Stewart was the bass, Mike Bryan was on guitar, and his big band had a very good pianist named Charlie Queener.

FRED: Fortunately you made some great records . . . *Slipped Disc, Rachel's Dream, After You're Gone* . . . lots more.

TEDDY: And there was a singer Goodman had in those days that to me is one of the greatest singers I've ever heard. Her name was Kay Penton. She didn't ever appreciate her great talent. Benny did, and I used to play accompaniment for singers auditioning with Benny and very often he wouldn't even listen to them after ten bars or so, but Kay Penton, he kept her singing for about an hour, just for his own pleasure, when he first heard her. Dinah Shore told me she auditioned for Benny once and he didn't even listen to her! That may have been one of the best things that ever happened to her, because she didn't become a big band singer and she's still a big star on television.

FRED: You played a number of the Jazz Festival venues, Teddy. I certainly remember you at Newport.

TEDDY: I've been at Newport since the beginning in 1954. I must have played twenty Newports. The promoter, George Wien, was an old associate of mine. When George was in college he used to come down to New York and study with me when I was teaching at Julliard. He didn't know what kind of career he wanted to go into. I think he had a choice of becoming a pharmacist, a doctor, but he loved the piano. One thing about George, he's been very successful in the business end of music, but he's playing now ten times better than he was in those days.

FRED: What's your life style these days, Teddy? You work just as hard as you want to?

TEDDY: I live on the road. I work from one job to another and in between the bookings I'm either in New Jersey or Boston.

FRED: You have a son who is in music, don't you?

TEDDY: Yeah, I have three boys. My trio now consists of my oldest son, Theodore, on bass, a younger boy, Steven, on the drums and then I have another son who just graduated last year from Ohio State and he's a pianist and he has his own TV show in Columbus, Ohio.

FRED: Well, lucky for us you're still playing, and if I may say so, better than ever, Teddy.

TEDDY: Oh, thank you. Well, I've kept right at it over the years, Fred, and I've spent a lot of time and lots of money to learn how to play the piano. I've been around some of the finest, besides Art Tatum . . . he was tops for me . . . but I've been around classical people. I spent a lot of time with Leonard Bernstein years ago, before he became famous as a conductor. I've been with some of the finest teachers. I would seek out Fats every time I could, when I was in the same town he was and, in Chicago, every night I was free I was at the Grand Terrace to listen to Earl Hines. So behind it wasn't any kind of thing like, "I woke up today and I could play just as a gift from God," or something! I have worked at this thing just like classical players and spent a lifetime at it. It's my hobby and it's my profession.

FRED: What's your advice to the young performer today, the one who is probably a graduate of Julliard or Rochester or North Texas State and probably has a great classical training. Does he need to woodshed?

TEDDY: There's two ways you can go to make a success, to me. You can go the studio route where you become a very fine, all-around player in different styles and you can learn to read music like the average person can read a newspaper. The other way is to do it like I do, we go for the **name**. We develop one style and promote our name to be associated with one way of playing. That's what the jazz stars do. To do that, you got to get on records, you got to circulate around and travel and get plenty of publicity to make a success, this path. Of course there's a third way, too—be a great club date player. These are the fellers who do the weekend work, who can play an Italian wedding, a Jewish wedding, a Greek wedding. They can play a little jazz. They can play a little Latin music. They can do any kind of party. They can play at the White House. Those who do that well, make a lot of money. Of course, if you're a very creative person, very often you don't have to do any of that. Your own creativeness just leads you. You just follow that, and sooner or later the right people will discover and it all takes place normally and naturally.

FRED: All I ask is, please, don't **you** stop.

TEDDY: I can't. I can't afford to stop!

Teddy Wilson

ALVINO REY and the KING SISTERS, 1940.
(Alvino Rey collection)

82

5

ALVINO REY AND THE KING SISTERS

William King Driggs and his wife Pearl had eight kids. Six of them were girls and each of the six became, at one time or another, part of "The Four King Sisters." Alvin Henry McBurney came out of San Francisco by way of Cleveland and changed his name to a more promotable "Alvino Rey" while he was with the Horace Heidt Orchestra. "Rey" translates to "King" and, fortuitously, the King sisters were also with the Heidt troupe, then riding high on radio and records. Luise King and Alvino fell in love, were married and when in late 1990, as I wrote these notes, were still a living example of just how good a marriage can be. They were far from retired, as you will see.

The King sisters were a star-turn before Alvino formed his first big band in 1939 and, with the band, went on to surmount all manner of professional adversity to become one of the most successful performing ensembles in the history of the Big Bands. Recordings like *Tiger Rag, Idaho, On The Alamo, Nighty Night* and so many others, were models of fine musicianship and innovative talent. The soloists, sidemen and arrangers were names to be reckoned with. Players, including Skeets Herfurt,

Alvino Rey

Herbie Steward, Al Cohn, Hal McCusick and Zoot Sims on reeds, Buddy Cole and Rocky Coluccio on piano; Don Lamond, Davey Tough and Andy Russell (soon to become a singing star) on drums; Chuck Peterson, Roger Ellick and Johnny Mandel in the brass section; and, out front, the only guitarist to lead a big band, Alvino Rey—all gave the band an exuberant sense of swing. To top it all, arrangers included Frank De Vol, Billy May, Bud Estes, Dean Kinkaid and Nelson Riddle.

The music world we remember in these pages was filled largely by **very** nice people. Among the nicest was Alvino. Unassuming, ever-considerate, fair and decent to all, he became a model of what a band leader should be. That included the required ambition, drive and dedication needed to cope with a world in which promoters, managers, record companies and other money-only people were too often unprincipled with a credo that seemed to say, "Money doesn't really mean anything to these musicians, they play for fun, anyway." Alvino's guys did enjoy what they did, that's pretty obvious from their recordings. The careers of the band and the Kings steadily rose until World War II shut down the band and many members, including Alvino and Frank De Vol went to work for Lockheed in Burbank and later into the Armed Services.

Post-war, Alvino reorganized and put together a sonic spectacular that included **six** trumpets, four trombones, five saxes and the usual three rhythm, plus Alvino. The recordings of that period on Capitol and Hindsight (originally radio transcriptions) show that the Rey band could out-blow even the Stan Kenton power-house when it chose to do so. There have been many Alvino Rey bands since. I had the good fortune to book several to play dance dates for my radio stations through the years and Alvino and Luise became our friends and neighbors in Southern California's Ventura County. He and I had much the same background as life-long radio hams and electronic bugs and that helped solidify our friendship. Later, the Reys moved back to Utah and we continued to stay in touch. My wife and I were among the first to hear Alvino's current jazz group perform. The King Sisters, meanwhile, had become, with other members of the extended King family, major stars of TV and records. The youngest sister, Marilyn, will sketch-in the beginnings of this one-of-a-kind musical family for us.

MARILYN: It started with my father who was the son of one of the pioneers across the plains. Daddy was in Utah and decided, he was going to be a great musician. He was self taught, studied all by himself. He finally went to Brigham Young University in Utah for a couple of years and then he said, "I'm going to be an opera star" and went to Chicago but gave up. He fell in love with Mother and they had one baby and another baby and another baby and another baby and another baby (laughter). So he gave up trying to make a living and decided to put his children to work. He took them all over the Midwest as a vaudeville group with instruments playing in churches and theatres. Then, from that, several of the girls decided to form a trio. They had a radio show on KSL in Salt Lake city. Horace Heidt came through and said, "I would like you to join our band, come to San Francisco" and that's where they went. I think that was in the 30s and that's where Luise met Alvino Rey. He was the guitarist with the band. They fell in love and got married and...

FRED: His real name is McBurney or something like that.

MARILYN: Yes, Alvin Henry McBurney. He's Scotch.

FRED: Right.

MARILYN: But they formed their own band and started recording in the 40s. That was really the beginning of vocal group times, when there was, what, The Rhythm Boys?

FRED: The Mills Brothers, The Rhythm Boys, ...

MARILYN: The King Sisters, The Andrews Sisters...

FRED: There could be no more difference than what existed between the Andrew Sisters and the King Sisters, except they both did Swing.

MARILYN: Right!

FRED: An entirely different approach to harmony, it seems to me.

MARILYN: Oh, completely! And I was wondering where my sisters got it. They just made it up. They faked it. They didn't read music at that time. But naturally, when they started doing records and from the 40s, 50s and 60s on, then they worked with all the great arrangers in the world.

FRED: Who dropped out for you to come in?

MARILYN: Donna had five children and she got a little tired of trying to take care of five children and being on the road so I took her place. So I've actually been with the group since the late 50s.

FRED: You must have taken some time off, you've got a couple of kids of your own.

MARILYN: Yes, I have three children. I never dropped out. I worked until I was 8 1/2 months pregnant each time.

FRED: Holy Smoke!

MARILYN: On the road, one nighters, the whole bit.

AUTHOR'S NOTE: The saga continues as we turn to sister Luise King and her husband Alvino Rey and interviews which took place over many years, through late 1990.

FRED: Luise, did the sisters, when they began, take inspiration from any of the other singing groups like the Boswell Sisters or the Andrews Sisters?

LUISE: Well, the Boswell Sisters are **really** our idols. That's how we got started. We used to hock every penny we had and buy their records. We kind of took over their job, they were singing at San Francisco NBC and they left and got a commercial, Chesterfield or something, really big time and went to New York City. NBC was looking for a girls' trio and we went up there and auditioned for their spot. We copied everything they did. They probably were our major influence. And then later on, I would say, when we got into the four-part harmony, I think it was The Merry Macs.

FRED: What an extraordinarily talented bunch of guys, and too often neglected today on records and not remembered as well as they should have been. Well, the Sisters as a quartet did very well from the very beginning.

LUISE: When we first started out with *In the Mood* and a few things like that, we had no idea and were really innocent about the money that could be made on records. After about six months or maybe it was a year, we got this letter from RCA. We looked at the check and it said five and we thought maybe $50, then we thought well maybe it's $500, and then it turned out to be **$5,000** and we screamed and jumped up and down. And you know what we did? We all went out and bought ourselves a mink coat. It was the first bit of luxury that we ever had, Boy, we were the happiest little gals you ever saw. We didn't know what we were getting into, you know.

FRED: Let's go back to the early days with Horace Heidt. Which of the King Sisters were together at that time?

LUISE: Maxine, Alyce and I were singing with Horace Heidt. Maxine married a young man who lived in California. She went East with us for awhile, but she got very homesick for her young husband so she retired and came home. Then Yvonne and Donna joined us and we became a quartet. It was probably the first girl quartet.

FRED: Four-part harmony.

LUISE: We kind of pioneered four-part harmony. We created a lot of things that the Andrews stole from us. We were kind of dumb, but very creative. The Andrews Sisters made a big hit out of *Scrub Me Momma With A Boogie Beat* after we had made a cute arrangement of the *Irish Washerwoman* but used the boogie treatment. The Andrews Sisters heard us and they swiped it from us and changed the name. We had an arrangement of *I Think I'm Going Out of My Head*. And the. . .what do you call them, Alvino?

FRED: Oh, you mean The Lettermen!

LUISE: The Lettermen, yeah! They came in and they listened to us and said, "Boy, I sure like that arrangement of *Going Out Of My Head.*" The next thing we knew they had made a big hit out of it.

FRED: They are still singing it and have been calling themselves Reunion now.

LUISE: Alyce's boy sings with them. He's in the film business, but on weekends and now and then he sings with the Reunions.

FRED: Alvino, first of all, how did you get into the music business and did you always play guitar? And, what made you decide to, of all things, play the steel guitar in a swing band?

ALVINO: I started out on the banjo, when that's all that was in a band was banjo. In the 20s, you know. And then I heard a wonderful guitarist in Cleveland, Jack Rose, and I got influenced with that and started taking lessons from him. And then I heard Segovia's records in 1928. That gave me another approach to loving the guitar versus the banjo. Of course, then the banjo was going out and guitarist Eddie Lang came into the picture. I became an admirer of his. Bill Madden, a violinist who was the Concert Meister of the Cleveland Symphony loved jazz fiddle, so he and I became a team like Venuti and Lang and went to New York. We joined Phil Spitalny's orchestra and went to the Pennsylvania Hotel, following people like George Olsen.

We were there two years and, of course, the first person I went to look up was Eddie Lang. I got my first guitar from him which I still have. We became friends, real good friends until he died when he was with Bing Crosby. There were no guitars playing in New York. I didn't find any other guitars. I used to go up every week and jam at Harlem, but there was never a guitar player until George Van Eps came along and we both studied from the same teacher in New York. That was the beginning of the guitars. Years later Dick McDonough and Carl Kress came into town and they all started playing guitar then, but when I went to New York, there were no guitar players.

FRED: When did you get involved with the steel guitar?

ALVINO: I had no interest in the Hawaiian guitar. It was a very simple melody thing. It didn't have chords. I was fascinated with harmony and so, to make a long story short, I heard on the radio a guitar tuned in an interesting way. The guitar player was a saxophone player, Andy Senella, the lead alto studio player that played all the staff stuff in New York. He played this guitar tuned to a seventh chord which was unheard of in the Hawaiian field.

LUISE: Very modern!

ALVINO: Well, at least it was an offshoot from plain simple triads that the Hawaiians used. So I got myself a guitar and tuned it that way. When I quit New York after the big crash, we went to San Francisco and I became staff guitarist and banjoist at KGO, which was the head studio for NBC on the West Coast. In those days there were no amplified instruments and we had a program every week on NBC called "A Bridge To Dreamland" with Paul Carson on organ and myself on steel guitar. It became very popular. Even today I run into some people who still remember it. And then we ran across an electric attachment for guitars and applied that to the steel. That made a big difference. At least we got sustained notes and we could play up with the volume of any of the other instruments in the band. And then, as the years went on we tried to add attachments to make the chords better, and all of a sudden we had a good arranger. He said, "Well, why don't you tune it like the big bands do now with the big brass section." So we added a couple more strings and imitated the brass and that's how we got the imitation of eight brass instruments. And each year we'd add more strings and add more chords and then added foot pedals to change and alter the harmonic structure of the guitar. That was in the mid '30s and, of course, by '40 we had, I thought, a different sound for an orchestra.

FRED: Has your design for the guitar been used by other people since?

ALVINO: Oh, yeah, there's a million of 'em out now. Mainly the country players use them. They don't want to be called Western anymore because they are making too much money.

FRED: That's for sure.

ALVINO: They call themselves Country which I still don't like.

FRED: Looking back in history a little bit, you started with the Horace Heidt band, didn't you?

ALVINO: Yes, that was in Chicago at the Drake Hotel. We had the Stewart-Warner Program in those days.

FRED: As a matter of fact, I always thought that Horace Heidt's band was pretty corny, but he was a great showman, and he spawned an awful lot of good people.

ALVINO: Yes, but De Vol was in that band. That's when we knew he could arrange. Later, we hired Frank from a little Hawaiian band in Philadelphia.

FRED: And Frankie Carle was in the Heidt band too, I think.

ALVINO: Yes, he followed me when I left the band.

FRED: What finally made the opportunity available for you to make the break and put together a group of your own?

ALVINO: Well, the King Sisters came out to California, that being their home. My home was San Francisco. They got some offers to record for Bluebird Records and they asked me to accompany them. Then we had an offer to go to the Mutual Network where I was program conductor for a year or so. That's how we started really, we started on the radio.

FRED: And your big band then, started in '39?

ALVINO: Yeh, '39, August '39.

FRED: And you did your own booking in the beginning?

ALVINO: Well, we auditioned for MCA. I thought it was a great audition. They said it was very nice, but we never heard from them. So then we booked ourselves. The first date we had was in Pasadena, I think it was 4,000 people. But the reason they came was because they'd heard us on the Mutual Network every night. We were on five nights a week. We became infatuated with the sound of the big bands that were coming to life like Miller and Benny Goodman. So we thought we'd go to New York and start over because we felt California wasn't the place for that. And so we broke up the band. We had a seven year contract with Mutual which I sort of regret leaving, but then the King Sisters, myself, Skeets Herfurt, and Buddy Cole went to New York. We reorganized and rehearsed and got a wonderful band and went to work. We had transcriptions which were getting all over the country and we had a little following. So we went to Hartford, Connecticut, to play. They had heard our transcriptions so they hired us at a beat-up old amusement park called Capitol Park Casino. We went there and **no one** came to see us. There was nobody.

We got paid off in spaghetti, no money. So here we are, after Frank De Vol writing all the great things, the King Sisters and all, and we're doing four full shows and all kinds of stuff. We were destitute then. We didn't know what to do. So, a friend of mine who had booked us there says, "I'll get you five one nighters" and I think two or three of those checks bounced and we were about ready to give up. The girls wanted to go home to mama! And then we had a last minute call from a place in New Jersey called The Rustic Cabin. They had a punk kid singing there, Frank Sinatra. I think he got, for three nights, $5. He waited on tables and sang. They decided to put a band in there and we stayed two years with three networks, the Blue and the Red and I guess Mutual, I don't remember. And that's where we sort of got our start and that's when we started recording in New York for Victor and Bluebird.

FRED: I well remember the radio broadcasts from The Rustic Cabin. It seems to me that one night you were snowed in and did a broadcast anyway?

ALVINO: Yeh, two people came in on skis. Those were our only customers for the evening.

FRED: But the engineer couldn't show up.

ALVINO: Oh, yeh, Charlie Kibling, who was one of the engineers, did the whole thing. He'd come in, unlock the mixer and put it out, put the mikes up, and do the announcing and all. Of course, we knew what he did, we knew the thing backwards. He couldn't get through the six feet of snow.

FRED: So you took over the engineer's duties. You were engineer and announcer and leader of the band and guitar soloist all wrapped up in one. The band must have gone through a lot of changes in personnel during that period of time. You and Charlie Spivak, I think, were rivals in terms of trying to grab the best musicians.

ALVINO: He was across at the Glen Island Casino.

FRED: I well remember that.

ALVINO: At that time you couldn't get the good drummers and all the good lead trumpet players, so you'd offer them a couple dollars more and you'd lose them once in a while. Very seldom though, théy were generally pretty loyal. They liked the band. Money didn't count.

FRED: The overhead, Alvino, in a band in 1940, for example— what kind of a payroll did you need compared to today?

ALVINO: Well, we started out with $28 a week, didn't we Luise? And, ah, I think the highest paid man was $50 a week. I think we stole him from Les Brown. Les Brown was starting about the same time we were. And then he stole our drummer or lead trumpet player and then Charlie Spivak came into the picture and he took our good drummer away. I remember, we got our drummer from—we stole one drummer from Les Brown, Eddie Julian, and then we got the drummer from Tommy Dorsey, and then Charlie Spivak stole him.

FRED: Quite a game! It must have been a very casual sort of thing at that time!

ALVINO: Money was not at all the main interest. The side men wanted to play with the band because they had good arrangements. They weren't concerned with money at all, it seems. After the war they **were** concerned with money and then they weren't very cooperative from then on. And the price would then about quadruple. $300 or $400 was a drop in the bucket.

LUISE: We noticed a great change right after the war in musicians— in their feelings, you know. The boys that served in the war felt that they had missed out on making money during these years, so they hiked up their prices. It was an entirely different feeling. Before the war everything was just so beautiful as far as money goes. Nobody cared. They just wanted to have fun and play. That's why the band was so great. I think that was the downfall of bands a little bit after the war, because they all got money hungry, like everybody else.

FRED: As I recall, The Rustic Cabin in terms of miles wasn't very far from Frank Dailey's Meadowbrook, was it?

ALVINO: No, about 15 miles.

FRED: Right, and they were competitors.

ALVINO: Yes. At that time we couldn't get into Frank Dailey's because we hadn't been heard on network radio so we took the next best thing which was The Rustic Cabin. Later on, we went with Frank and he loved the band so much he wanted to manage it.

FRED: But we're getting a little ahead of our story because that happened after the band really hit its stride in New York City. That first engagement there, I am told was a disaster. It was at the Biltmore and weren't you in Detroit at the Jefferson Beach when the Biltmore sent somebody out to audition the band?

ALVINO: Yep! We were doing wonderful, business was great. A Biltmore rep came to hear us and was very impressed with the business we were doing so they hired us to go into the Biltmore, thinking we would be a society band like Horace Heidt. We were thrilled to go there. In the meantime we had six brass and a pretty roaring band. We had to play soft so we put mutes in and played real soft. Of course, all the executives from the big companies would come in with their...

FRED: ... to talk business...

ALVINO: ...and to talk business they didn't want to be disturbed by a noisy band. But if they had their spouses with them, or whoever, they'd come and dance to us. That went on fine except the band itself was very unhappy because we didn't want to play music like Eddie Duchin and all those bands. So one night a friend of ours had heard a radio transcription and came up and asked us to play *Tiger Rag*. So we said, "What the hell" and took the mutes out and blasted out *Tiger Rag*. Everyone in the room was astounded and the manager of the hotel came up in his nightgown and robe and told us to get out and that was the end of the Biltmore.

FRED: Of all the hotels or dance hall venues that you played through the years, which ones did you find most congenial and where did you have the longest runs, Alvino?

ALVINO: Well, I think the Astor in New York and the College Inn in Chicago were the best places with the band and the ones who appreciated us the most. We'd go back there year after year. In fact, we made the Astor our home. We had an office there and loved the New York people and enjoyed that, and also Chicago. We loved Chicago. Then, as we got farther West, we weren't too interested. The people weren't with it out West when we were there. They've all moved out here now but...The Palladium, yeh, you'd go in there for a couple of weeks and all the movie stars would come in and Tommy Dorsey would be there, but that was it. No one even wanted to do one nighters on the West Coast. They loved the one nighters in New England and Pennsylvania and Ohio. In fact the biggest business we ever did was through Ohio. It was wonderful. I never felt that about the West, and besides when you jumped from Denver and had to go all the way, 700 miles, to the West Coast, it was tough.

ALVINO REY and his Orchestra at the Rustic Cabin in New Jersey, 1940. (Alvino Rey collection)

LUISE: Those days we felt that the kids were much hipper in the East than in the West.

FRED: These days you play a lot of engagements in Florida. Is that partly because there are so many fine musicians to work with down there?

ALVINO: They've all moved down from New York. There's no place in New York to play so they've got Disney World to play, you know. And then, of course, the Jewish clientele are wonderful people for an audience. They understand music and they understand comedy and see, they've all moved and retired to Florida and so, when you play for them you really have an appreciative, understanding group.

FRED: Luise, I think about 41 members of the King family were involved one way or another in the King Family television show that ran so long on ABC TV. How did that come about?

LUISE: That started out as a benefit. Our sister called up the family. We always got together at Thanksgiving and Christmas time and my father, being a vocalist and everything, would say, "Well, come on, let's sing a song." We'd sit down at the Thanksgiving table and we'd sing almost as much as we'd eat, and that's quite a bit. We had some wonderful times. Speaking of the family and getting the whole family together, Vonne said, "Would you come up and do this church benefit?" Everybody said, "I don't know." But they did. She said, "Oh, you can all stay at my house and we'll have a ball!" So we all went up. The whole family, the kids and the husbands and everything. The benefit turned out to be so good that the people from ABC saw it and they made a Kinescope of it. They bought it as a special and it went on from there.

FRED: You and Alvino are living in Sandy, Utah, now and you venture out on concerts and dance dates and other things once in a while and you often sing with the band. Tell me about your sisters. Where are they now?

LUISE: Alyce is in North Hollywood and just plain being a Grandma and enjoying her home.

FRED: Who is she married to?

LUISE: Robert Clarke, the actor.

FRED: How about Vonne?

LUISE: Now, Vonne has moved up to Sacramento where Tina, her daughter, is living. Tina, you know, besides being one of the stars of the King Family Show, was in My Three Sons with Fred MacMurray.

FRED: Then there is Donna.

LUISE: Donna! Donna is living in Woodland Hills with Jim Conklin who was President, you know, of...

FRED: Capital Records?

LUISE: Warner Brothers, I'm sure you know, and then Capital Records and Columbia Records. She has five children kind of scattered all around. She is very... we've always kidded about Donna, she's always been president of women's clubs and is very active lecturing and just having a great time.

FRED: Your youngest sister, Marilyn, who joined the King Sisters in the 1950s, is still very active I know and has made albums on her own. She has a family, too.

LUISE: She has a daughter, Suzanna, who is living in Connecticut with her husband who owns a TV station. Marilyn is doing promo things where she writes them and sings them for radio.

FRED: She's also done some nightclub appearances, hasn't she?

LUISE: Oh, she always has. She's always gone on by herself.

FRED: So, she's still singing?

LUISE: Yeh. She's still singing.

FRED: Okay, now let's see, have I left out anybody? Any other sisters that filled in?

LUISE: Maxine, the elder sister who retired started out singing as a trio when we first started.

FRED: Did you do your own arrangements in the beginning?

LUISE: That's our problem, we love chords. I tell the story that we very seldom fight about anything. The only fights we have are musical fights because one girl likes one chord and another girl likes another chord.

FRED: Were you all trained musically?

LUISE: Yeh. We'd sit around with an arranger like Billy May or Frank De Vol or Ralph Carmichael. We've had some great arrangers who would sit patiently with us. We would say, "Now, we want to do this, and we want to do that," and we would always have our foot in arrangements, you know. They were half ours and the arrangers would help us.

FRED: Are your own kids carrying on the musical tradition?

LUISE: We have we think, a very talented Liza who is kind of pioneering with the harp. She seems to have the talent of Alvino, but she plays the harp and plays swing, rock, or very wild music. She also plays symphony music. She's a schooled musician. She is making quite a name for herself in Houston, Texas, playing the night clubs and jazz joints and things like that, and doing concerts. And our boy does gigs but he works for. . .

FRED: Robbie?

LUISE: Robbie, our oldest boy. He is talented but he came along when the music business was kind of going out. So he works for the post office now but he still writes and enjoys a little music. Our other boy, John, is a businessman, but he is talented. He sings and plays the guitar and stuff like that. Neither one of them went into music.

FRED: Okay. Alvino, what are you doing now? You are working with a friend, a fine pianist. Tell me about it.

ALVINO: We have a great jazz quartet. We're very excited about it, and, when we play a jazz festival, it's been very successful. We just finished rehearsing today and Bob, who is such a genius, comes up with very wonderful ideas.

LUISE: Bob Bailey.

ALVINO: We're very content with this. I've also been playing colleges. I send them the arrangements and then I sit in and play the guitar with them and I give 'em a symposium lecture on the band business, jazz from the beginning, which I really grew up with. And that's been very successful. First, we'll do an hour concert with a small group, the quartet, and then we'll go into an hour concert with the big band.

FRED: You also do concerts with symphony orchestras, I know.

ALVINO: Well, you started it. You did our first concert in Ventura, right?

FRED: Right! With the Ventura County Symphony.

ALVINO: Then we played Salt Lake and. . .

LUISE: Nashville.

ALVINO: . . .and Baltimore and different places around.

FRED: So, you're both staying very active, there's no question about that.

ALVINO: Oh, we're still interested in and excited about the business. You know, the big band thing has sort of gone by the wayside, but the jazz thing is sort of kicking over and the festivals are a pleasure to be at. That's about it.

FRED: That's enough. Well, how about the hamming. You still busy with that?

ALVINO: Oh, every day, you bet. One every day. If you'd get your license back we'd have a little QSO once in awhile.

FRED: Tell me your call letters, I forget.

ALVINO: W6UK, W6 Uniform Kilo.

FRED: Boy, that goes back. The call letters now are so many variations I've lost track of how they are doing it now. You've held on to that for how long, Alvino?

ALVINO: 70 years!

FRED: Holy Smoke!

ALVINO: I have my gold certificate sitting in front of me here.

LUISE: He was the youngest ham. He was eight years old when he got his license.

FRED: How many are there in the King family today do you suppose?

LUISE: Well, we had a family reunion last summer. We have them every other summer and there were over 100. Half of them I didn't know. Seems like the King Sisters didn't have a big batch of kids. We had three or four kids each. But all of **our** kids are having big, big families. So it's really a mob.

AUTHOR'S NOTE: The full history of this colorful family has been recorded by Luise in two beautifully written books. These, along with a great many recordings of the King Sisters and Alvino Rey, are available directly from Luise and Alvino. Write them at Post Office Box 321, Sandy, Utah 84070. They'll be delighted to hear from you.

6

HERB JEFFRIES REMEMBERS
THE DUKE

In late May of 1980 I was asked to present Herb Jeffries with a long-delayed Gold Record of his 1941 hit, *Flamingo*. By that time we had lost Duke Ellington, with whom Herb had made that memorable side. By 1988, when I brought Herb to perform at a jazz concert at the famed Ranch House Restaurant in Ojai, California, Herb was the **only** remaining member of the historic 1941-43 Ellington band. Herb had been a single performer for forty-five years and, in fact, in 1990, as I prepared this for publication, he was still appearing on stages and in clubs all over the world, still in fine voice and performing with drama, intensity and good humor. His memories of Ellington as he reminisced with me seemed to catch the essence of Ellington the man and the greatest band he ever had, one of the greatest the world has ever known. Consider just some of the sidemen—Brass: Rex Stewart, Cootie Williams, Juan Tizol, Lawrence Brown; Reeds: Johnny Hodges, Barney Bigard, Ben Webster, Otto Hardwick, Harry Carney; Rhythm: Sonny Greer, Jimmy Blanton, Fred Guy; Piano: Duke Ellington, Billy Strayhorn.

"Mr. Flamingo," HERB JEFFRIES, circa 1950.
(Ray Avery photo)

Here's what Herb says about that extraordinary orchestra:

HERB: It was a university of music within itself, a traveling university and each man was picked because he was a graduate of life. The Professor Ellington who selected you, he was the Dean and he selected each individual because he felt they had graduated somewhere along the line in the school of hard knocks and you became a member of his university. Everybody that came into contact with this man, he uniquely sculptured them. He turned them around into what he saw. You know, a block of clay that a sculptor picks. The true sculptor who innovates from his mind says, "I have a block of clay and inside of that block of clay is a figure and I'm just gonna dig away at that clay until I dig that figure out. They don't know what it's gonna be." Ellington was that way with music. Many nights I sat with him and watched him sculpture music, but I also watched him sculpture people. He would pick them and they were a block of clay. He saw inside of that person each unique individual. This man had an all-star band. Every person that he picked was unique in his own right. You know, you talk about Hodges. Where is there another Hodges, ever, ever?

FRED: Harry Carney or Cootie Williams or any of those people.

HERB: Never, ever, ever, one in a life time like your fingerprint.

FRED: When did you join the band?

HERB: You know, Ellington was such a clever man. He had an idea in his mind and he wanted to test it out. And I was in Detroit at that time, working, and he came in the club and he heard me sing and about six weeks later I got a wire to join him in Indianapolis. I went to the Lyric Theater in Indianapolis and I stayed with them for that engagement at the Lyric. I think this was about a week and then it was, "Thank you very much," and I came back to Detroit. And that was in 1939. Then I came to California and got involved in the motion picture business and made a lot of Western pictures—did some Western recordings.

FRED: I didn't know that.

HERB: Yeah, did a lot of cowboy songs and Western songs and Western folk songs and then I did four Western pictures out here and one of those pictures was very successful for me. Then I went back to Detroit. "The prodigal son returns" with the cowboy hat and the boots and the whole thing because I did some Western things that allowed me to do that. And I went to the Graystone Ballroom in Detroit. Ellington was playing there. He had played at the Apollo Theater with one of my pictures which was called *The Bronze Buckaroo*, and he called me up on the stage, introduced me. I did some songs with him, it was in early 1940, and he said, "What are your plans?" And I said, "Well, I guess I'll be going back to California, do some more cowboy pictures." He said, "Oh, what a shame, I was gonna ask you to join the band." I said, "Well, I think we can put those pictures in the background for a while."

So I joined his band in early 1940. In late 1940 on December the 28th in Chicago I did a song called *Flamingo* written by a man by the name of Ted Grouya and Ed Anderson. It was recorded but not released until 1941. And, of course, like most records, as you well know, it's roulette and it's the greatest gambling game in the world, records. The difference is that in Las Vegas they play with small black chips and the record business plays with them big ones. In those days were the ten inch chips we played with and it got lucky. The number hit and we had a hit record.

FRED: I wonder how Ellington happened to pick that particular tune. It was not one of his own and it was very much off-beat, a little Juan Tizolish, maybe.

HERB: Yes. Well, you know, a funny thing is, when we were playing in Jersey this Frenchman by the name of Ted Grouya came backstage to speak with Ellington. Duke was busy in a meeting at that time and he said, "Go downstairs and take a listen to a song—they're ballads, and see if there's anything this guy's got that you might like." So I went down to rehearsal hall and I heard several of his tunes and the *Flamingo* tune sort of appealed to me. When I went back up and spoke to him he said,

"Did you like anything?" I said, "Yeah, the guy left me a copy of it." And he said, "Give it to Strayhorn and let's see if Strayhorn likes it and you go over it and if it's any good maybe we'll do it on our stage shows and give it a test." He was a very clever man. He would take songs and he would test them on the stage performances. If the audience reaction was really high, it was sort of his testing ground as whether it was worth recording or not. And we got such a tremendous reaction from our stage performances that he called me in and said, "We're gonna record this number."

FRED: Johnny Hodges didn't hurt either.

HERB: No, Hodges and neither did Lawrence Brown who played a trombone solo in that too.

FRED: That had to be, in that period of time up through about 1943, the very greatest of the Ellington bands.

HERB: Yes. Actually, I think that was the apex of all of his pickings throughout the time of the orchestra. It was a phenomenal orchestra. I can remember Jimmy Blanton being with the band and he was a young lad that Duke found when we were in St. Louis. Ellington was a great guy to wander around in the late hours of the morning and he would go to the after-hours spots and hang-outs. He was a great hang-out guy. He found a lot of talent that way and a lot of songs. He would hang out—he loved to hang out.

FRED: Let's talk about some of the soloists from the band and your impression of them, Johnny Hodges, for example.

HERB: The Rabbit? Yeah, Hodges was a unique character. He was not a Mr. Personality. He was very laid back and quiet like. I guess all of his emotions went into playing the music, playing the horn. Although he and I got along very, very good. He was very protective towards me because I was the young one in the band and he was always giving me advice as what to do and so on.

FRED: Ben Webster.

HERB: Ben Webster was the roughneck of the band. He could get very physical if something upset him. Of course, not ever with the band did he have a disturbance. But I have seen him outside of the band get tough in nightclubs with people and, you know, threaten to throw them out the window or whatever. He was very protective over Jimmy Blanton.

FRED: Jimmy Blanton, of course, was the great bassist who died all too young and he really changed the whole sound of the band, didn't he, the part that the bass plays in big bands?

HERB: Yes. Well, you see, prior to Jimmy was Baud. Baud, of course, was always just a great foundation for Ellington's primativa and he was great and played a huge, a humongous bass. And, of course, when Blanton came into the band—there's no question about it—the whole personality of the band and its sound changed, yes.

FRED: Barney Bigard also should be remembered as a composer. As a matter of fact, did Ellington get credit for some of the things that Barney wrote?

HERB: Well, Ellington was a great business man and what Duke would do—just remember that the foundation of the band was there with Ellington's creativity and his arrangements, but what some of the great men that he picked would do would be to take his melodic line and innovate off of it or do more or less an obligato to his melodic line. But Ellington's ear was so sharp when he heard a passage on obligato that was repeated several times, then he would create a melody out of it and then he would go over to the musician and say to him, "Me and you, we're going to write this together." And then he would take that obligato that was played against it and create a melodic line out of it. He did that with Toby Hardwick in *Sophisticated Lady* and in many things that Barney did. But they got paid or got credit for it, yes.

FRED: Was Harry Carney the unsung hero of the band?

HERB: I think Harry Carney was the catalyst. He was without a questionable doubt the catalyst in the band. He was the guy who kept that sound constant and solid and secure. He was a most fantastic musician, and I doubt very much whether anybody will ever play that instrument, the bass baritone saxophone, better than he, ever.

FRED: Rex Stewart.

HERB: Rex Stewart—roly poly, a very jovial guy who added a lot of comedy to the band because it was a very serious band and Rex gave us some joy and comedy in the band. He was the humor for our orchestra.

FRED: How was the esprit de corps? I have heard stories of the band showing up late on the stand with maybe just the rhythm section for a while and some of the instruments gradually showing up. Is that just fable or some fact?

HERB: No, there were times when that happened. That happens in all bands. However, Ellington, being again, the great genius and diplomat, would make it look as if that's the way it was done, see. So when guys would come late he would start on time and then he'd go out there with a small group and, as they would straggle in, it looked like you were compounding it all the time, see—adding a little bit more, a little something to it. And finally when it worked that way then he made it an invention. Then he would do it that way, see.

FRED: You know, RCA has been releasing all of those records from 1940, '41 and '42. Things like *Ko-Ko, Morning Glory, Concerto for Cootie, Me and You*, and *I Got It Bad and That Ain't Good* with Ivie Anderson, classics like *Cotton Tail* and *Dusk* and *Bojangles* and *In A Mellow Tone* and *Warm Valley* and *Jump for Joy* and *I Don't Know What Kind of Blues I Got With You, C Jam Blues, Perdido, Take the A Train*. They're all on a three CD set and RCA really cleaned up the sound for CDs too, sounds just great. And they call it the Blanton Webster Band which shows you the influence that both Ben Webster and Jimmy Blanton had on the band at that period of time. Jimmy died way too young, didn't he? He was 21 when he joined the band and I think he died two years later.

HERB: You know, isn't that interesting? It's true.

FRED: Like Charlie Christian.

HERB: Like Christian, yes, and like George Gershwin. But you know, I realize that it is not the length of life, but it is how much life you have lived in the time, how much you have produced in the time that you have lived. Guys like Gershwin, in the short life he lived, produced things that men who could live a thousand years could not produce. And men like Jimmy Blanton and Charlie Christian who have given a contribution to our being and to our life and times, things that if other men could live hundreds of years couldn't give us, you see. So it's not the length of life nor its height.

Ellington, who lived so deep and who somehow was chosen to have my path cross with this master, that I could serve as an apprentice with him and to have had that moment in time to color my life. And you know, God, what a privilege. What a great privilege to have been able to have passed with this great master who has given so much. My God, his compositions alone, Fred. You know, it's ridiculous, the compositions of this man. A thousand years from today people will be speaking about Ellington like they did Mozart, Beethoven and you know, the great masters.

FRED: Yet, we hear that his control of the band was a very casual, a very loose sort of a thing.

HERB: Yeah, you see, he did not have a kind of a command over his aggregation. But he had such an unbelievable respect by people who were in awe of his genius that he could be gentle and that gentle sensitivity had an effect on everybody. And so it is true that he wasn't concerned about that kind of discipline. He was more concerned with talent and ability, and he felt that people who had talent, uniqueness, must be given the privilege of not having to be disciplined.

FRED: Among your records a favorite of mine is *I Don't Know What Kind of Blues I Got.* Remember that?

HERB: Oh, indeed I do. That was kind of a unique thing because it really wasn't supposed to have had a vocal on it at all.

It was sort of an instrumental and overnight Ellington could get an idea and the next day he might come in and change the whole formula and say, "Well, okay, I want you to sing this." And if you remember the record, it was instrumental for a long time and then all of a sudden, for some unknown reason, a vocalist came in there and started singing something—Snake Mary. Snake Mary was the star in this 32-bar opera.

FRED: Sure, the lines went like, "There's no rest for the weary, I'm gonna see Snake Mary 'cause I don't know what kind of blues I got."

HERB: Really, if you looked at the things that this man produced, he produced short, short, short, short stories with musical backgrounds.

FRED: Speaking of short, short stories, I remember at a benefit performance for the society of singers in Hollywood a couple of years ago, I heard you tell of your personal struggle to form and shape your interpretation of *Flamingo*.

HERB: A funny thing about this song, you know, if you've ever seen a flamingo on picture postcards, you'll notice that they're always standing in tall grass. If you've been on those boats to the Caribbean, you know, down there on the flamingo farm, they have the tall grass for these birds to stand in to be comfortable. What you don't know is that I researched this song before I recorded it. I got special permission to fly all the way to Hialeah and stand in the pond there for about three months. That's true. And I got to know a little bit about flamingos. They want you to do that so that when you sing this song you'll have some feeling about what's going on with it. They did that with Brando *On The Waterfront*, you know. He had to spend some time on the waterfront.

Well, after about three months with those birds out there in the middle of that racetrack, nobody ever paid any attention to me then. They didn't pay much attention to the flamingos either because you know how race people are. But you see, wherever you see these birds you'll always see them in tall grass. Now what

109

you don't know is at Hialeah, that when all had left the race-track, including the maintenance people, and in the tranquility of that evening sunset and that magenta moon when the sun is going down, these birds smoke this grass. That's what makes them fly so high.

FRED: Herb, I would think that one of the musical highlights of your lifetime had to be your participation in Duke Ellington's show *Jump For Joy* which, as I recall, opened in Los Angeles in the summer of 1941 and never did make it to Broadway. It was a great show. It introduced, of course, the title song, *Jump for Joy* and most of all *I Got It Bad And That Ain't Good* and a lot of other wonderful songs. Ellington, I know, used to say afterwards—he had an objective in doing this show—that it had a message and that was to take Uncle Tom out of the theater, to eliminate the stereotyped image that had been exploited by Hollywood and Broadway about blacks and black music. Why didn't the show succeed in terms of going on to Broadway and having a long run?

HERB: It had a lot of problems. Like in anything else, what makes Sammy run? And what makes Sammy run is finance. We had good finance out here in California. As a matter of fact, we had too many chefs. I think at that time we had maybe seven different people who were financing the show and when you get that many chefs it becomes highly complex and there was trouble and arguments. Unfortunately, because of financial problems, it couldn't survive.

FRED: The next thing I remember about you is that sensational record of *Basin Street Blues*. With Buddy Baker, was it?

HERB: With Buddy Baker, yes. All the vendors of New Orleans. Leon Renee, who was the producer of that album, who incidentally is from New Orleans, conceived the idea to do the vendors in the beginning of it. It was that uniqueness in the production that made that record a success.

FRED: You've made a great many records over the years for various labels. I know you did one of old Nat King Cole songs and one of songs associated with Bing Crosby. Lovely albums. And also you did a song with Abez.

HERB: Eden Abez. When Abi brought that song *Nature Boy* to me long before Nat King Cole did it, the Musicians Union was on strike.

FRED: '43?

HERB: That's right. And so we recorded it, but we recorded it with a group of singers and it was done a cappella. It did all right. It went out and it did fair. I guess probably it made enough money to pay off the investment. But Nat King Cole came out with it and Nat had the big success, which he deserved because he did a magnificent job of it. I don't think anybody could have done as well with that song as Nat did. Many times I looked back and I said, "Gee, I'm glad that Nat finally came and recorded this number because I loved it so much, I don't think that I could have done the job that Nat did with it. It was right for him."

FRED: And the time was right for that song, too. How about today? Is this a time in which we are likely to see a resurgence of good music? In the personal appearances I've done and in the letters I get from listeners, including a lot of young listeners, I've noted that there is a resurgence of interest in real jazz and big bands and great ballad songs. You find that encouraging?

HERB: Yes. I love it. I love it because I feel that the wheel turns and I've seen it turn, you know, because, well, I've been around about 125 years now—well, 127 years. God, I hope that's gonna be true. I'd like to watch all the things that go on in this life. I really hope that I can hang in there that long. But anyway, back to where we were starting, I love it and I think it's great. I had an experience last night. A young lad came over to me and said, "Can I speak to you for a minute?" after I finished my show. "Can I have about 10 seconds?" I said, "Sure." He took me back in the room and he says, "Please," he said, "Where in the world have you been? Where can we hear this kind of music?" He said, "You know, I have people my age that are dying to hear music like this." He said, "We love it," and, "Where are you gonna be appearing and where can I come and hear you again and do you record and where can I get ahold of some records of yours?" It was really thrilling to me to know that there are young people around 25, 26 years old who dig this music. See, jazz is an American heritage. This is music that was born in this country and people all over the world in Japan, in Sweden, in Denmark, in France, in England who know more about American jazz musicians than our American kids do and this is our heritage.

This music was born in this country. And boy, it just makes me feel absolutely beautiful that today there is a maturity that is happening amongst our youth. And they are smart, they are beautiful. They are alert and they are vibrant people of America who are gonna run this country and are gonna take it to its Utopia because what has been happening to it now in the cultural arts is pathetic. We are suffering as Americans from cultural anemia. I'm sorry to have to say that, but it is true. But thank God there are youth like this young lad who came over to me who are exuberant and excited and boy, that is my hope. You know, I say, "Oh, God, isn't it great. There is somebody out there. They're not escapists. They don't have to go out there and listen to a lot of noises that are not really, truly sane sounds." I understand why they've had to have that. I understand that we've gone through a kind of an emotional stress that the entire earth has had and we've had to find something to keep us emotionally stable to go into.

FRED: Herb, you're a very emotional singer. A lot of drama goes into everything that you do. Does part of that come out of your experience with Duke Ellington?

HERB: If ever a man was cloned, Ellington cloned me. He inspired me in just about everything—his dress—I loved the way he dressed. I loved his discipline, a very disciplined man. His philosophy was beautiful which shows itself up in his sacred concerts. A very godly man. I was very much influenced by that. He was articulate. I loved his way of being articulate. He also was a great put-on. He loved to put his audience on. Sometimes he would come out and create and coin words that sounded like

DUKE ELLINGTON'S Band with HERB JEFFRIES at the microphone. 1941. (Ray Averys Jazz Archives)

gibberish and the audience was not sure whether they were in the dictionary or not and he loved doing that. I loved his kind of humor that he used, and so I find that in my performances, when I see myself on film or hear myself on tape, I hear Ellington.

FRED: You're happy with your life these days?

HERB: Oh, I'm totally thrilled with my life these days. When I open my eyes every morning and I see light I say, "Hey, it's good, I made it, and there's something out there for me to do." And as long as I have consciousness, it's a new beginning for me and so I'm very happy with my life. I've been hanging in here for a long, long time and I haven't been forgotten—that's neat. I started in—well, the flamingo flew in 1941 and most people come to this planet by stork and I came by flamingo.

7

JOHNNY GREEN

Of all the great standard American popular songs, *Stardust* and *Body and Soul* are likely the most recorded. Everyone knows Hoagy Carmichael wrote the *Stardust* melody and almost everybody knows Hoagy from his many recordings and films. But the composer of *Body and Soul* was Johnny (later dignified to John) Green, certainly no retiring, self-effacing fellow, but not a performer whose face the general public could identify as a star. But a star he was. Composer of *Out of Nowhere, I Cover The Waterfront, Coquette, I Wanna Be Loved, Easy Come, Easy Go* and many more evergreens, Johnny was a very fine pianist, who led his own orchestra on radio, for movies, and in the great hotels for many years. He was a formidable conductor of symphony orchestras and for MGM studios where he was the Executive-in-charge-of-music for many years, winning five Academy Awards for such films as *An American in Paris* and *Easter Parade*.

Johnny was a companion, an associate and a favorite of musical royalty. His career is a microcosm of the most creative, glamorous and productive period in American musical history, from the late 20s to the late 60s. As a businessman, Johnny

115

Green led the powerful American Association of Composers and Publishers (ASCAP) through some of its fiercest conflicts with broadcasters, recording companies and other major users of music. He could also deliver a half-hour speech for an hour, or two hours at the drop of a half-note and with the greatest of charm.

In the Spring of 1988, as I finalized plans to produce a "Tribute to ASCAP Composers" for my summer jazz series at the Ranch House in Ojai, California, I telephoned Johnny. He was an ASCAP past-president and I wanted him to be our guest of honor. "I'll be there if I can drag myself out of this bed," he told me. I learned he was gravely ill and died before the concert could be staged. This interview, however, took place in happier times beside his pool at his gracious home in Beverly Hills in January of 1986. As we began, I noted that Johnny, unlike so many fellow hit-makers such as Harry Warren and Sammy Fain, was not self-taught but instead was a Harvard graduate and had received an extensive musical education.

JOHNNY: Don't forget, I had my first big number one national hit while I was still in college. By that time I had written a large quantity of the world's **worst** chamber music, when I wrote *Coquette*. So, of the two ways that I burst—maybe burst is a little bloated—emerged on the scene in a kind of national sense, one was as an arranger...

FRED: This was for Guy Lombardo?

JOHNNY: That was my first paid professional job. And I hasten to add, I had nothing to do with formulating the style of that band; not that I didn't love working with the Lombardos, 'cause I did. But in those days there was the Gold Coast Orchestra at Harvard and there was the Barbary Coast Orchestra at Dartmouth and the Casa Loma Orchestra was a college orchestra. The Gold Coast Orchestra at Harvard, of which I was a founding member and the chief arranger, was so good that it made some records for Columbia, you know. So, my emergence into where people said, "Who is this fellow Green?" was by way of a popular song and arranging for dance bands. I think my point of view is not all that foreign from when you mention Harry Warren and Sammy Fain. Harry and Sammy are two of the most musically gifted men I have ever known in my life. It isn't important whether Harry Warren could give you the anatomical structure of a chord that he used. Nobody who sings *About a Quarter To Nine* or *Atchison, Topeka and Santa Fe* or *You'll Never Know* or any of those great Harry Warren songs gives a continental damn if Harry knows the difference between an appoggiatura and a Neopolitan six.

And as far as Sammy is concerned—funny you mention Sammy—because my first job, as they say in the movies, and I was a hot twenty years old, because as long as we're talking about me (my favorite topic), I graduated from Harvard when I was nineteen, so at the age of twenty I was working for Paramount at their studios in Astoria, Long Island, and Sammy Fain was working there. As the chips fell, I became two things; I became Sammy's orchestrator and musical secretary. I never found either job beneath my dignity. I loved working with Sammy and I'll tell you one of the proud small medals that I wear is that the first time the American public ever heard *You Brought a New Kind of Love To Me* by Sammy and Irving Kahal, they heard it in my arrangement and orchestration in a picture called *The Big Pond* starring Maurice Chevalier. That's what Sammy wrote songs for. I was the orchestrator of that picture.

FRED: You wrote *Coquette* before you were with Lombardo. Did he introduce the song?

JOHNNY: Yes, he did. It was just a tune that I brought with me when I went to Cleveland. I came to Lombardo by way of those very Columbia recordings that I mentioned earlier. Guy heard them and was intrigued with what he heard and made it his business to find out who had written those orchestrations and who was "little old me." Guy got in touch with me at Harvard and asked me if I'd like to work for him that coming summer, which was the summer between my junior and senior years. A

117

close, close, close friend of the Lombardos was the king of popular lyricists, Gus Kahn. I had a lot of melodies that I took with me to Cleveland, and one of them was the one that we are talking about, and the Lombardo boys liked it. But Carmen (Lombardo) thought there were things about it that should be different. That's why you see Carmen's name on the music. That's the only song of mine in which I ever had a collaborator, but *Coquette* is by Johnny Green and Carmen Lombardo. The song took its shape, its form, in which you know it, during that summer of 1927 and Gus Kahn was out there visiting the Lombardos and Gus fell in love with the tune. Gus gave it the title *Coquette*. Gus was the king of Leo Feist. You may remember—I hate to date you, Fred, but you remember the logo, "You can't go wrong with a Leo Feist song." Well, they were my first publishers, thanks to Gus Kahn. The song was published in September of my senior year and by January it was number one.

FRED: Your song *Body and Soul* arguably is the best song you've ever written, but you may not agree with that.

JOHNNY: Well, I ain't ashamed of it.

FRED: I understand that it was difficult to convince publishers and performers in this country to use the song. They felt that perhaps it was a little too complicated, so you went to England with it?

JOHNNY: What happened was this, Fred. During the period that I wrote *Body and Soul* with Eddie Heyman, I was Gertrude Lawrence's accompanist, or if you'd like it a little more earthy, I was Gertrude Lawrence's piano player. Maybe a few of our audience would drop a quick, "Who was Gertrude Lawrence?" Gertrude Lawrence was the first lady of the British stage from mid-twenties through the initial run of "The King and I" in which she played Anna in New York. Well, I had met Gertie Lawrence while I was still in high school, and that's a long story. I fell out with my father, who didn't want me to be a musician, which is why I'm a graduate Harvard economist (may the dear Lord help me). I went to work in a Wall Street bond house when I graduated from college, all of this to please my dad whom I loved very much, a brilliant man. I didn't agree with him about much but I loved him and I recognized his great brilliance. In any case, I walked out of that Wall Street bond house job after six months and said, "What am I doing here, this isn't what God wanted me to do with my life." That caused a big rift with my old man and I needed a job. And who gave me my job? Gertie Lawrence! And just as today, if Ann-Margaret's going to have a new act in Las Vegas, Marvin Hamlisch writes the new act.

Gertie Lawrence in those days not only appeared in musical comedy and in legitimate theater, but she appeared in what the British called cabaret and she appeared in what the British called the wireless and she made what the British called gramophone records. She wanted some special material so she commissioned Eddie and me to write four special pieces. Well, if you were writing a clump of four pieces of special material for that kind of a performer, what would you write? You would write a rhythm song, you'd write what we call a comedy number but the British call a point number. You'd write a lovely (God willing) ballad, and in those days, the inevitable torch song.

FRED: Which was, of course, *Body and Soul*. I know the show opened in England and it seems to me that the first big hit was by the famous Bert Ambrose Orchestra.

JOHNNY: Bert Ambrose was home dressing to go to the evening session at the Mayfair where he played with the Ambrose Orchestra. He had his wireless on and he heard Gertie Lawrence singing this song he'd never heard before. He rushed to the phone and got Gertie on the phone and said, "What is that song? That *Body and Soul*, who wrote it?" She said, "Johnny Green." He said, "Our Johnny Green, our *Coquette* Johnny Green?" She said, "Yes, the same." He said, "Well, how do you come by it?" She said, "He wrote it for me." Well, I will make it very brief from here, she gave him a manuscript copy that she had—overnight he had one of his guys do a "scratch," as we call them. The next night he started playing it at the Mayfair and it was unprecedented. Every band in London, every artist in London was coming in and taking it down—that is literally true.

It spread like wildfire and the next thing, I got a call from the late Henry Spitzer at Harms. He said, "Did you and Heyman write a song called *Body and Soul?*" I said, "Yeah, we wrote it for Gertie Lawrence." He said, "Are you aware what a smash it is in England?" I said, "Well, I heard that she did it and that some people were playing it." You know, I was so naive at that point, it's hard to believe, but I was. Anyway, he slapped a contract on Eddie Heyman and me and it was published in England, not in this country. It became, I don't mean to sound egotistical, it became the anthem of Europe. As a result, Max Gordon bought the American rights to a song written by an American composer and American lyricist that had become an English song. He bought the American rights for Libby Holman in the show *Three's a Crowd* which starred Fred Allen, Libby Holman and Clifton Webb and opened in 1931. Libby Holman introduced it to this country.

FRED: If I had to choose a favorite recording of that song it would have to be Coleman Hawkins' *Body and Soul* without any singing. What would you say, Johnny? With all the records made, it's probably the most recorded song of all time.

JOHNNY: Well, it's one of the most recorded songs of all time, one of the, I guess, three or four of all time. Coleman and I were good friends and you know, that recording, that treatment of *Body and Soul* is a classic and I loved it. On the other hand, it is a jazz treatment and the very essence of jazz is improvisation; that's the heart of jazz, that's it's motivation, that's it's genre, that's why it exists. So what you have on the Coleman Hawkins record is very little of the theme and an awful lot of the variations, if you want to use the nomenclature of the classic form of theme and variation.

FRED: But the changes are intact and the song is unmistakable on that account.

JOHNNY: There's no question about it, but it's Coleman Hawkins superimposed on Johnny Green, if you will. I would think even though Ella Fitzgerald also goes off into other spheres, she really states the song and she sings the lyric. I think maybe that's my favorite recording.

FRED: Let me jump around a little bit. I guess my second favorite of yours is *I Cover The Waterfront*. Did that come out of a picture also, Johnny?

JOHNNY: No, it went **into** a picture. I'm being only a little facetious. You know that picture came into being as the result of a series of stories in the New Yorker Magazine by a waterfront reporter by the name of Max Miller. Max Miller wrote this series of articles or stories in the New Yorker and the byline of his column in whichever New York paper it was, was, "I Cover the Waterfront." He was a maritime reporter and also a great short story writer. That was the inspiration for the picture. I don't remember who did the screen play. Edward Small produced the picture and it was called "I Cover The Waterfront" and it starred Claudette Colbert and Ben Lyon. There was a guy, a very enterprising, bright, bright young man with United Artists by the name of Monroe Greenthal and we are talking 1933. Eddie and I by that time, you'll forgive me, were hot as a pistol. We were very famous, we had *Out of Nowhere*, we had *Body and Soul*, we were doing nicely, and Monroe Greenthal wanted an exploitation song for the picture. This was very early in the days of exploitation songs.

So he called Eddie and me in and offered us a very handsome stipend to write this exploitation song. Well, to be an exploitation song for the picture it had to have the title of the picture. He had ordered a ballad because he figured that it had to be a ballad because it was a love story and he wanted it to reach the hearts of the public. I didn't want to do it. I said, "What kind of a title is that for a love song? *I Cover the Waterfront And That's Why I Love You*?" But my beloved Eddie Heyman, he said, "I think I can lick it." That was enough for me, if Eddie thought he could lick it. I said, "Eddie, you're the doctor." And did he ever. I mean, you only have to think of the first couple of lines of that verse that Eddie wrote: "Away from the city that hurts and mocks, I'm standing alone by the desolate docks, in the still and the chill of the night." Do I have to go any further? It's one of the great song poems ever written. In the refrain, the chorus: "I cover the waterfront, I'm watching the sea. Will the one I love be coming back to me?" That's it!

FRED: So he did the lyrics first in this one instance.

JOHNNY: He came up with the first line of the verse and the first quatrain of the chorus, I then went away and wrote the music and we worked together from there. But I mean, it's sheer poetry, but I wouldn't have done it and it was one of the biggest songs I ever had.

FRED: Again, what's your favorite recording?

JOHNNY: I think Sinatra's, I really do.

FRED: There's a great instrumental on it, of course, Artie Shaw.

JOHNNY: Artie and I were talking—sitting here talking on the eighteenth of January. Less than a month ago. I had a long, long talk with Artie. If Artie likes you, you can't have a short talk with Artie.

FRED: Artie's a friend of ours and Gita (my wife) has been working on some of his songs. She said, "Writing lyrics to some of his tunes, he'll call up and say, 'Look, I've only got a minute here and I've got eighty-nine things to do,' and an hour and a half later. . ." As Mel Torme said, "The trouble is that you take a breath when you're talking to Artie, forget it, you'll never speak again."

JOHNNY: Oh yeah, but he's fascinating. The first record that I made for Columbia with my first band called *A New Moon Is Over My Shoulder*, well you know every record, opens with a long clarinet solo by whom? Artie Shaw.

FRED: That's a record I wish I had. The only records of your big band I really have or that I can get my fingers on are the ones with Fred Astaire.

JOHNNY: Well, I'll settle for that.

FRED: Those were records you can say were perfect in every detail.

JOHNNY: What an extravagant compliment! Well, they are archival. I'm very, very proud because they're all my arrangements, you know.

FRED: And featuring your piano.

JOHNNY: Yes, and one of the very proud things in my life, Fred, is the number of treatises about those recordings, that have been written around the world, in Germany, France and England. They really are a block of archival stature. And, of course, I loved working with Fred.

FRED: And you worked with him a lot. Didn't you do the Packard Hour with him on radio?

JOHNNY: I did the Packard Hour on radio and I worked with him at Metro, of course.

FRED: I made a note of two of those records that I liked best, *They Can't Take That Away From Me,* and *The Way You Look Tonight.*

JOHNNY: Those are two of that series of recordings that are very close to my heart for very sentimental reasons. Don't forget that those records were made at a time when we still recorded on the big, thick, soft wax and on a slave turntable and instant acetate was turning. Those acetates really shouldn't happen to Hitler, they were so awful, but there was no such thing as tape, so there was no editing. You started with groove one and it went through the last cutoff. That was that take. Both George Gershwin—my life was infinitely blessed because both George and Jerome (Jerry) Kern were close, close friends of mine. When I got the rough pressing, it was two days after we had done the recording on *The Way You Look Tonight,* I rushed out to Jerry's house (Beverly Hills) with it and said, "Here" (I'm going to choke up.). He sat there and cried like a baby and came across the room and put his arms around me and gave me such a hug, and exactly the same thing happened with George in *They Can't*

Johnny Green

Take That Away From Me. But it was the same scene and I can still feel those two hugs and I can still see those two guys with the tears coming down their faces. I feel blessed that God gave it to me to write those arrangements because I adore those two songs.

FRED: You worked with Fred on at least two movies that I know of. I wonder how it was to work with Irving Berlin? I've always heard that he was on the set all of the time and had his finger in everything that happened.

JOHNNY: Irving was a professional curmudgeon, you know. I had a great experience with him on *Easter Parade* because our contract with him at Metro called for him to write four new songs for the picture. We had the rights to all of the Berlin catalog. By we, I mean MGM. You know nobody ever created a note for Irving Berlin, you take my word for it, but on the other hand, he was a complete illiterate musically. He can only play in one key, depending on which way you are looking at the piano, it's either F-Sharp major or minor, or G-flat major or minor. You know about his piano where he could clamp the keyboard around—why did he want that piano? Because his ear is so sophisticated that he hears other keys, he hears the entire spectrum of the harmonic language. He's brilliantly gifted.

His musical right hand is a guy called Helmy Kresa, who worked with Irving on everything for years. Helmy was sick at the time. I mean not a cold, he was seriously ill, at the time that we did *Easter Parade* and unavailable to help and Irving was beside himself. He was frantic because he had to write these four songs and somebody had to put them down 'cause he didn't know how. So I was music director of the picture and I said, "Irving, who can be Helmy Kresa? If you would accept me I would be delighted to **try** to be Helmy Kresa." Irving was so darling about this, "Holy Christmas, the great Johnny Green is going to sit and take down while I play?" I said, "The great Johnny Green could learn something. Please, Irving, it would be a privilege." He couldn't get over that and he slapped his knee—you know the great Berlin gesture. I did learn and I learned plenty.

I have to tell you an anecdote which you will love. In one of the songs I took down, I sat there in a chair and he's at the piano playing in F-sharp. I sat down with my pad of manuscript paper and I took the song down. I said, "Gee, that's a nice song, Irving, this song, you know. I have one thought." He was avidly interested, he wanted to know. I said, "In such and such a bar, Irving, you played the third in the bass and it has a somewhat muddy sound." I hadn't gone near the piano yet, and I figure we'd be better with a fifth in the bass in that particular spot. He said, "Let me hear it, let me hear it, I want to hear it." So I went to the piano and he said, "Now play it my way first." So I played it his way. "Now play it your way." I played it my way. "Play it my way again." So I played it his way again. "I like my way." And that was it.

I have to tell you another story. He had written a score for Fred Astaire called *Follow the Fleet* in which there was the song called *Let Yourself Go* and we recorded it, Fred and I. The arrangement opened with a big poundingly rhythmic and very complex, mind you I did not say complicated, I said complex, big difference, piano solo. Irving Berlin blew his mind about that piano solo. He called me on the long distance phone and he raved about it and so on. But he said, "Who was playing the other piano?" I said, "What other piano?" He said, "That's two pianos." I said, "No it isn't,Irving." He said, "I never thought I'd live to see the day when you'd lie to me." I said, "Irving, that's God's gospel truth." "I don't believe you," he said and he hung up. Now he bet Jerry Kern or told Jerry Kern about it and Jerry Kern said, "Irving don't sell Johnny short. Playing piano is one of Johnny's businesses, he's very damn good," said Jerry who told me all about this.

Irving bet him $500 that it was two pianos. Long dissolve and there's a big dinner in Irving's honor at the Ambassador and who is the music of the evening? Johnny Green and his piano and his orchestra. Irving said to me at the beginning of the evening

"You going to play *Let Yourself Go*?" I said, "Sure I am." He said, "You're not afraid of getting caught in your lie?" I said, "You and your calumnies, you are the liar." He said, "I bet Kern $500 that that's two pianos." I said, "Well I hope you got $500 on you," because Kern was there too. He said, "I want to come over and watch when you play it." So he made a whole big thing of it. We played it and there I am, it is a very digital piano solo, I can still play it. Can I say on this microphone what Irving said?

FRED: Sure.

JOHNNY: He said, "Well I'll be a son-of-a-bitch." He said, "God damn you, Green, you just cost me $500." I said, "I never enjoyed $500 more in my life, pay Kern." And he took out a wad of bills and he paid Jerry Kern the $500.

FRED: You are the only composer I can think of off-hand who wrote a call and response series of songs, one was *I'm Yours* and the other was *You're Mine, You*. Were they done close to the same time? Which came first?

JOHNNY: *I'm Yours. I'm Yours* I wrote during that period at Astoria. There was another moderately gifted songwriter. Obviously I'm being arch when I say **moderately** gifted, there at one and the same time at Astoria. I'm going to leave me completely out of it. Working there on staff was Sammy Fain, Irving Kahal, E. Y. Harburg (otherwise known as Yip), and a fellow with a little talent called Vernon Duke. We were all there together at the same time. So Yip and I wrote a lot of stuff together. *I'm Yours* was Yip's first big hit. None of the other things I wrote with Yip ever exploded outside of the matrix in the pictures they were used in, but that's when that song hit. It was written for a short. Those were the days when shorts were a very, very important part of motion picture theater programming. There was a comedian called Lester Allen who wore an on-purpose ill fitting tail coat with a black tie. I got to tell you, there are people today who wear a black tie with a tail coat. I find it very offensive, but anyway, Lester Allen had the tail coat that dragged on the floor (laughs) and the vest came down to his crotch, and he wore big shoes. You know, the floppy clown type shoes. And the name of this short—actually it was a featurette—most shorts were two reelers and they made featurettes that were four reelers, and this was a four reel featurette called *Leave It To Lester.* Yip and I wrote *I'm Yours* for that.

FRED: You know I'd like to talk to you about the pictures, your tenure at MGM, but that would take us another couple of hours.

JOHNNY: That's another interview.

FRED: I do want to touch on a couple of pictures, one that you got an Oscar for, *An American in Paris,* working with Gene Kelly and Oscar Levant and all those good people. An inspired film from beginning to end. I wondered how anything that good could have come out of a major studio.

JOHNNY: Oh, Fred, that's the first—you know this is the first time we've done an in-depth interview together—but knowing your work and you and your points of view for a long time, how could you say that about MGM? We did fabulous things at MGM. All the calumnies that have been heaped on L. B. Mayer, he was one of the great master showmen of all time. Think of the people, Sidney Franklin, Sam Zimbalist, Clarence Brown, William Wellman, the directors who were under contract at MGM. That's the greatest stock company that was ever assembled in the history of entertainment going back to the days of Aeschylus, says he, being pontifical. But it's true and that word-wise-fumbling, loose-coin-jingling fellow called Arthur Freed was one of the most divinely gifted men who ever lived.

To work in the Freed unit was Elysium. You stop to think, the team that made *An American in Paris.* Let's start first of all with the Gershwin catalog at our disposal, that's the starter. Second was the still healthy, vibrant, virile, strong, interested, mentally alert Ira Gershwin as part of the team; Vincent Minnelli in his prime as a director; Irene Sharaff in her prime as the costume designer; Allen Jay Lerner, before he got artsy-craftsy, as the screen play writer; John Green (forgive me, cause I was the head), Saul Chaplin and Connie Salazar as the music team and Cedric Gibbons as the Art Director with Arthur's concept.

"Body and Soul" composer JOHNNY GREEN at the piano. MGM studios, 1950. (Ray Avery photo)

Arthur's concept was using the late impressionists as the sets for the ballet. And, of course you mentioned, Gene Kelly, that's one of the most creative minds that God ever put on the face of the earth. That was the team that made that picture, how could it not be great?

FRED: Let me just get you to analyze one particular routine, *I Got Rhythm* done so differently for those little kids, a whole different approach. Was that Gene's idea?

JOHNNY: Yes. Gene's idea and my orchestration.

FRED: One of the last original movie musicals was a wonderful picture called *High Society* with a score by Cole Porter, with Louis Armstrong and the band, Frank Sinatra, Bing Crosby, Celeste Holm, and Grace Kelly, of course. And you were the music director.

JOHNNY: Well, that was another one of my joyous times although that was the picture on which Frank and I had the feud. Our relationship has never been the same since. He wrote about it in his book, that one book of his. And I must say, he told it as it happened. I got sick and tired of Frank conducting for me on the recording stage. You know how, in the operating room the so-called scrubs, terrible word, the scrub nurses would slap the tools in the surgeon's hand, and by reflex he grabs it? That's what I did with the stick. I slapped the stick in Sinatra's hand and I walked off the stage. A stupid thing for me to do, arrogant, stupid, pompous, pig-headed, egotistical. I'm a nicer fellow today. I spoiled a very beautiful relationship. I know Frank has never forgiven me for that. He's right. No! He's not right. It's never right not to forgive, but that's another story. That's where I turn my collar around backwards.

FRED: Other than that, did you have fun on the picture?

JOHNNY: On *High Society*? Oh, of course, with Louis Armstrong and Grace Kelly. That's another one of my, I may-not-always-be-wrong-but-I'm-never-right, stories. I opposed Grace singing her own track in that. And Grace and I were good friends before that picture. I'd known Grace since she was a youngster and I didn't want her to hurt herself. I didn't want her to be hurt by doing it and then having us take the track out and doing it over again, with Bing and a double.

FRED: *True Love* was the song.

JOHNNY: Yes, *True Love*. She made a big issue of it. She went to Dore Schary and made a big issue of it, and I lost. And P.S., the record went to platinum.

FRED: Getting back to Johnny Green, the Composer, one of your songs that is most often played today, especially by jazz musicians, is *Out of Nowhere*. And again, Eddie Heyman wrote the lyrics. I know that this was composed around 1931 and much, much later it became a hit all over again in a new motion picture.

JOHNNY: That's another case. I don't know what it is, I seem to have been hexed lyrically, because here Eddie Heyman's lyrics to *Out of Nowhere*—course when I talk about Eddie I have difficulty with the lump in my throat because I loved him so, so dearly. He's gone now, but he made every hour as sweet as a flower for me. You don't think of an hour having a bouquet like a flower, but Eddie Heyman did. He was a poet. He was an earthly poet. Well, another man whom I deeply admire, Hal Wallis, was at the time of which I am about to speak a producer at Paramount. Of course, Paramount owns the song. Don't get me started on that! Don't get me on the subject of copyright or you'll do a series. But Paramount owns the song under the crazy copyright laws of this country, Paramount is the author-in-fact. You know about that? So they can turn it upside down, play it backwards, do anything they want with it.

Well, Hal Wallis was making a picture with Lizbeth Scott at Paramount and he was looking for a song to use as the theme for the picture. He didn't want to spend the money on commissioning anybody to write a song. Or maybe that's unfair, maybe it was Paramount that didn't want him to spend the money. In any case, he sent to the people in the Paramount Music Department to come in with all of the songs that they thought might be appropriate for that picture. Hal is a very, very smart fellow, a very great showman. He loves music and he knows a lot about songs and all. The name of the picture was *You Came Along*. And so he's listening to one song after another and he hears a song of which the opening phrase goes (sings) di-da-da-di. Being the creative producer, he's singing "You came along" and the next line is "from out of nowhere." Of course Eddie Heyman's line was "You came to me from out of nowhere." Well I'm doggoned if they didn't grab the song. That became the song.

But anyway the song, the picture was a big hit and the use of the song in the picture, whether it was called *Out of Nowhere* or *You Came Along,*gave the song a new lease on life. Eddie Heyman and I—I don't want to be gross enough to talk the actual figures—but the royalties we got from the shot in the arm given to it by Hal Wallis's use of it, were like six times the royalties we'd gotten in any like period for goodness knows how long. Eddie Heyman and I were absolutely outraged by this. My attorney, one of the great entertainment field attorneys in the world and of all time was Martin Gang, I hasten to add, another Harvard man. I went to Martin and I wanted to sue, and Eddie wanted to. So, Martin says to me, "What's the biggest royalty statement you've had from *Out of Nowhere* in any year since its first initial big year, since it became a standard? What's the biggest total income you and Eddie have had from *Out of Nowhere* in that period since then?" We told him. He said, "What was your last check?" We told him. It was, like six times bigger, more! It was a big, sizable chunk of money. He said, "And you want to sue them? Not only would you not get to stand up before the judge, they wouldn't let you in the courthouse!"

FRED: In recent years you've done more conducting, it seems to me, than anything else. Practically all of the major orchestras in the world, including the Los Angeles Philharmonic at the Hollywood Bowl, all say John Green instead of Johnny Green in the publicity releases and credits. Do you want people to call you Johnny or John?

JOHNNY: Well, I want people to call me what they are comfortable with. John is my name. I was Johnny, not only professionally but socially, for years. When I became Associate Conductor of the L. A. Philharmonic it was Mrs. Chandler's idea that Johnny wasn't elegant enough for the L. A. Philharmonic. That's how John came in.

FRED: What is it about harmonic structure of your songs, the songs that we've talked about here, that appeals to jazz musicians so much? Can you put a finger on it?

JOHNNY: I can't answer that modestly.

FRED: Wait! Nobody asked you to answer it modestly.

JOHNNY: Well, the dear Lord gave it to me to be inventive, tasteful and practical at the same time, harmonically speaking. I say so frequently, Fred, and I do want to get this in, I say, "Thank God." I don't do these things alone, Fred, none of us does. I mean, gifts come to us from the Almighty, I've always believed that, I just wanted to get that in. But people make such a big hullabaloo, you know, about the impossible difficulty of the middle of *Body and Soul*. Well, I didn't invent inharmonism. Inharmonism is when the key-tone of an outgoing musical statement becomes the leading tone into a new key a half-tone higher. I wrote *Body and Soul* in D-flat major, so that the key-tone of D-flat is obviously D-flat. The middle strain starts out in D-natural major which is a half-tone higher. Therefore, the key-tone of D-flat becomes what is called the leading tone, becomes a C-sharp leading to D-natural. I didn't invent inharmonism, but I happened to be the first pop songwriter to use it in a pop song. And then everything that happens throughout that middle is perfectly natural. It lies under the fingers.

I happen to be a saxophone player myself. You know about saxophones, you know about the thumb keys and the octave key and all. You don't have to go through any of those gyrations. Everything lies naturally, you see. So you say, "Why do jazz musicians like the way I write harmonically?" They also like another composer, harmonically as much as or better than I, that's Harold Arlen. He has the same gift, the same type of gift only much greater than mine. What we write is inventive but it's also in good taste. It's natural, it's musical. It is not, you know, putting your left elbow in your right ear. Or as we used to say, you don't go from New York to Boston by way of Philadelphia. You go up to Boston Post Road. That's the way my harmonies go.

FRED: Looking back at a career so full of so many different things, what part of it gave you the greatest satisfaction? What do you look back on with the greatest pleasure or sense of accomplishment? Writing songs? Leading a band? Playing the piano? Conducting? Scoring?

JOHNNY: I don't think I can be exclusive about that. I love making music and when I'm doing any one of the things that my so called versatility makes it possible for me to do, that's what I love most, when I'm doing it. And when I'm writing, I love writing most. When I'm conducting, I love conducting most. I love the theater. I love any time that what I'm doing musically is in the ambience or environment of the theater. And the theater means everything from a concert hall to the screen to the musical theater. I love being where there's a live audience that can applaud. I'm the world's biggest ham.

Johnny Green

8

LES BROWN

Writing about Les Brown in terms of his importance to the music of the 20th Century is much like writing about Felix Mendelssohn in the 19th Century. In each case, a happy childhood, encouraging parents, enormous natural talent and a sunny disposition has led to happy, uplifting music. In the case of Les Brown, it, together with some very good luck, has made him the sole surviving member of the leaders of the Big Band Era who is still leading a constant, fully-organized, never less-than-exciting dance band in the 1990s. That means more than half a century of demonstratively-successful leadership. I interviewed Les a number of times from 1977 through 1990 and found him always responsive and never controversial. Charming, hospitable, sure of his talent and of those he has chosen to work with him, Les has managed to avoid, again with some exceptional good luck, the many pitfalls and economic disasters that meant enforced retirement, if only temporary, for so many leaders.

Today, Les plays about 75 dances and concerts a year, using mostly musicians who have been with him for many years. He plays golf almost daily and bridge in between. He and J. Hill write virtually every new arrangement for the Band of Renown (named, as an ad-lib, by a radio announcer on a remote broadcast from Washington, D.C.). Les records new albums and enjoys a parade of great reissues from Columbia, MCA and other labels. His radio and TV shows with Bob Hope, Dean Martin and others, and his eighteen tours overseas into scary war zones with Hope have built for Les a constituency that won't quit. Fortunately, neither would **he** as the decade became the 90s. It all began in 1912 in Reinerton, Pennsylvania, with a baker-musician for a father.

FRED: Did you have formal, classical musical training after high school?

LES: Oh, I went to the Ithaca Conservatory of Music and studied under the great Patrick Conway. Three years of harmony, theory, arranging, the whole works and this was **before** I got my high school diploma. I went to Ithaca when I was too young to have finished high school and went to a military academy on a full scholarship, just to prep for college.

FRED: Why did you choose Duke University and wind up leading the Blue Devils band?

LES: There was already a Blue Devils band, two of them, actually. One was led by Johnny Long and one by a singer and football player named Nick Laney. I heard the Laney band the summer of 1927 when they were playing a gig up my way. One of the reasons I went to Duke was because I got free room and board just for playing in the band. That meant a lot during the Depression, I can tell you! Tuition for a year at Duke then, was only $300. When Laney graduated, or actually finished the four years of football they'd let him play, I took over the band.

FRED: There's a composite photograph of you and your wife, Cluny, over there on your piano—one a picture taken on your wedding day and one fifty years later. Amazing how little you both have changed! How did you meet your wife?

LES BROWN leads the famed Duke Blue Devils in 1936. Courtesy
Les Brown

LES BROWN BAND, New York City, August, 1941. Les on sax
(left), vocalist Betty Bonney on the piano, Joe DiMaggio (baseball
legend at her side) as band records its first hit, "Joltin Joe
DiMaggio."

LES: When the band left Duke as a complete unit in the summer of 1936, we spent the summer working at Budd Lake in New Jersey. That's when I first met her, but we didn't date, then. Two summers later we came back to play Budd Lake and there she was, still hanging around the bandstand. We fell in love and that was that.

FRED: And you have two kids, a daughter who now is in real estate, and your son, Les Junior.

LES: Who sings with the band. He plays drums, too, but he's usually too busy singing.

FRED: And what about your dad?

LES: My dad had the home town band wherever we went and he was sort of an itinerant baker, all in the same section though, of Tower City, Pennsylvania, which is about 30 miles from Pottsville. Then right next door was a little town called Williamstown in a different county but it was only about five miles away. Then five miles from Williamstown was another town called Lykens. He had bakeries in all those towns at different times. While he was there he was always the leader of the home town band.

FRED: A brass band? The kind that would perform in a park on a sunny afternoon?

LES: Yeah. A marching band more or less. They did some concerts, very few concerts. Played some overtures like "Poet and Peasant," things like that. But mainly Sousa marches and whatever were popular music things of the day.

FRED: What did he play?

LES: He was originally a trombone player but once he became leader he let that go to hell, so to speak.

FRED: Did he encourage you to get involved in music?

LES: Encourage me! He put me in the bake shop and said "practice!" and if he didn't hear any noise coming out of the bake shop he'd go and slap on the wall which means, "Come on, you're not practicing." Yeah, he was a Teutonic sort of person, I guess paterfamilias. He was the boss of the family and you did as he said.

FRED: Did he live to see your success in later years?

LES: Yes he did. He lived to be 92.

FRED: Wonderful! How did he feel in the early days about swing and jazz?

LES: Oh, he enjoyed that; in fact he had a dance band on the side. To raise money for the home town band they used to have square dancing and Dad played the drums in that. One of the boys in the bank would play the cornet, another the tuba, and Dad would play the drums. We didn't have a piano player, so we had to find one. There were no violinists in town, so I had to play the violin parts by transposing a note higher on the soprano sax to play for the dance jobs we did Saturday nights during the winter. I was about 12, 11 or 12 at the time.

FRED: You were still in short pants!

LES: Well, that brings up another story. One time when I was about nine, I was the only saxophone player in the town that could read music. So, I was hired by a dance band to play in some town about 30 miles away, and this was my first big gig and I didn't have any long pants. But there was a boy next door who was my pal who was about three years older than I. He was very short so I borrowed his long pants to wear to my first professional gig that I got paid for.

FRED: And in all the years that have followed you've been working steadily, leading a band.

LES: I had one year sabbatical you might call it. We left school in June of 1936 and went out on the road and worked for a year and three months, and then the boys in the band had parental pressure to get back in school, rightfully so. So, the Duke Blue Devils was disbanded in '37 and for a year I went into New York and worked as a freelance arranger before reorganizing in 1938.

FRED: Did you play a lot of clarinet in the earlier days of the band because that was the fashionable thing at that time?

LES: I led the Duke Blue Devils band I was in, with clarinet, because in 1934 when Benny Goodman became so popular, at least with musicians and then later on with the public, I gave up the tenor sax and stood up in front of the band with the clarinet. But I gave up playing long ago because if I couldn't play as well as Benny or Artie or Abe Most or Irving Fazola, and a few others I admired, I decided I'd better just stick to waving my arms and doing arrangements.

FRED: Well, even with your arrangements, the band in the early days on Decca Records and then RCA's Bluebird label, didn't sound much like it does today.

LES: Oh, my gosh, we were just out of college. We hadn't matured at all. In fact I'd like to buy all the masters and I hope they never re-release those.

FRED: And with Columbia the first hit was what, the *Jumping Joe Dimaggio* thing?

LES: First big hit, yeah. We had other things like *Bizet Has His Day* and *Mexican Hat Dance*, things like that.

FRED: Abe Most joined you about that time didn't he?

LES: Yes, he was with us then.

FRED: You had been doing the clarinet lead parts and Abe took over your solos.

LES: As soon as I got Abe, I stopped playing.

FRED: When did Doris Day join you? She was with you twice I think.

LES: She was with us twice, yeah. First in 1939 and then she got married and went back to Cincinnati, had a baby, got a divorce and she came back with us around the end of '42. She was with us until right before '47.

FRED: She came pretty intact didn't she, in terms of style?

LES: Oh, she's a natural. She sang so beautifully, her intonation, her sound, her natural swing. She could do anything—ballad, swing or *Que Sera*.

FRED: The big hit of course had to be *Sentimental Journey* and that was what, '45?

LES: It came out January '45, just as the war was being won. It was well timed, so to speak.

FRED: This was a piece of yours and Ben Homer?

LES: Ben Homer and I wrote the melody and Bud Green wrote the third lyric. Bud Green was the same guy that wrote *Once In A While* and *Flat Foot Floogie*, of all things. He did a great job.

FRED: Was it a surprise hit?

LES: No, we knew it was going to be a hit because we had been playing it at the Hotel Pennsylvania and people kept coming up and saying, "What is that, what is that?" And we couldn't record it because there was a recording ban on.

FRED: That's right.

LES: So when the ban was lifted in December '44 we went right in, recorded it, and it was released in January, and history!

FRED: You've been very lucky with gal singers, haven't you? Lucy Ann?

LES: Oh, Lucy Ann Polk was fine with us. Then there was Ray Kellogg's wife, Eileen Wilson. And now we've had Jo Ann Greer since then. She's been with us since the 50s.

FRED: Did you have male ballad singers with the band? Jack Haskell?

LES: Well, we had Jack Haskell. We had Hal Derwin and Gordon Polk. But none of them made any records. Ray Kellogg and Eileen Wilson got married while they were both on the band. But neither of them got to record anything that meant too much.

FRED: I thought Haskell was an especially good singer.

LES: He was!

FRED: Very, very smooth, easy.

LES: I first heard him when he was with WGN in Chicago and he had a 15-minute show out of there daily during the week. We were playing at the Blackhawk in Chicago. So I called him up to hire him to come with the band and he said, "Oh, thank you very much. It's very flattering but I go into the Navy next week." Of all things! I said "Well, call me up when you get out," and he joined the band after he got out of the Navy.

FRED: And then there's Butch Stone, singer and sax player and much more. He's very important to the band besides playing and singing.

LES: Greatest man I ever hired. He manages the band on the road and takes care of all the details that I don't have to worry about. My brother, Stumpy, now that Don Kramer has retired, is doing the booking. Between him and Butch, all I have to worry about is the music.

FRED: Talking to Van Alexander, he was telling me that it was his arrangement of *A Good Man Is Hard To Find* that finally turned up with you and with Butch. Butch had done it with his band and Butch had done it with Larry Clinton.

LES: Well, we recorded it in 1942, in fact, the first time we were at the Palladium. We recorded it again back in the '70s.

FRED: For the BASF label?

LES: Yes. "How Brown Sounds Now" is the name of the album.

FRED: And I think he also did *Leroy Brown* on that. You still do that don't you?

LES: Oh yes, that's one of his big ones because Butch dances around and we have the audience join in.

FRED: Here in California you sure don't have any problem finding musicians to back up long time Les Brown members like

Butch Stone. At least half the great players in the United States settled here to play in the studios, didn't they?

LES: That was one reason we changed venue right after the war. We came here in 1942 and played the Palladium for the first time, and made a movie at the same time. Boy, that was tough work!

FRED: What was the movie, by the way?

LES: *Seven Days Leave.* It was on television just last week. When we first came to California, my wife said, "This is nice, this is it, here's where we are coming after the war is over." And just before Christmas in 1946, I told the band in New York, "We're moving to California and if you want to come out, I'm going to take a few months off and reorganize in California and you'll all have a job if you want to come out there." We had a big party and there were a few tears around and things like that. We moved and some of the boys did come out there the following March. In March of '47 we opened at the Palladium and have been going ever since. That was the only break as far as the band was concerned, since October of 1938 when we opened in New York.

FRED: How do you account for the longevity that the band has had, considering that others have come and gone? Even Harry James and Count Basie for awhile had to give up a big band. How were you able to survive?

LES: We're lucky because we toured on a limited basis to begin with. When we joined Bob Hope in '47, that gave us a big advantage because we had a weekly radio show. Then television came along in the early '50s and we had radio and television. Then, of course the big radio shows became extinct, but we still had television. And, when Steve Allen moved out here in 1959, we did his show for two years. Then we did the Hollywood Palace, '62 I think it was and '63. For nine years we did the Dean Martin Show. So, we not only did dance work, but television work.

FRED: How did you get associated with Bob Hope? You're celebrating that anniversary, too.

LES: Forty-three years, yeah. We started with him in 1947. Well, we were at the Palladium and his radio agent—he was sort of split up— he had a movie agent, a radio agent, and a one- nighter personal appearance agent. Jimmy Saphier was his radio agent and of course Bob was very big in radio at the same time as were Jack Benny and Bing Crosby. They were the three Number Ones, taking turns being Number One for years on radio. We were playing the Palladium and Mr. Saphier sent up a note that he'd like to talk to me. He's an ex-trumpet player, by the way, and he just wanted to tell me how much he liked the band. So, I asked him, "Are you satisfied with your band leader?" and he says, "No, we're not, as a matter of fact." And I said, "Could I put in my application?" He said, "Oh, no, you can make much more money traveling." I said, "You said the magic word. I don't want to travel anymore. I just bought a house in Beverly Hills. I want to be in California and that's it." He says, "Well, give me your phone number." I heard from him the following week and we were hired. He took the records over to Bob Hope and hired us. He was also trying to sell Doris Day to Bob but he said, "No, I can't let Frances Langford go." Two years later Doris Day was with the Hope show with us on radio.

FRED: But you did a lot traveling with Hope all over the world. Did you ever count the mileage?

LES: Only at Christmas. We spent two weeks between December 15 and December 30 for about 18 years in a row.

FRED: Were those trips relatively uneventful or were there hairy times on some of the trips that you made?

LES: Oh, we had some close calls, I understand. I had to read about 'em because I don't remember 'em bein' that close. One time I was in a helicopter that had malfunctioned, with Jerry Colonna and Janis Paige and Barney McNulty, who was our idiot-card man. There were four of us and we were in a snow storm. We were going from Soule, Korea, up to the Bayonet Bowl and all at once we landed and I said to the pilot, "Is this where the show is?" and he said, "No, they're going to send a car that takes you the rest of the way." We found out later that the generator had gone and luckily he was low enough to glide down, and that got a lot of publicity. None of us were perturbed because we didn't know what was happening.

FRED: How did they treat you, in general, on those trips?

LES: Oh, like royalty. They were so happy to have us.

FRED: You could not have had a more enthusiastic audience, I would think.

LES: Best in the world. They were starved for any kind of state-side entertainment, including, of course—he always brought a lot of pretty girls, for which he got a lot of criticism from some people, but they liked it.

FRED: Oh, yeah! The GIs sure liked it. Eighteen trips starting when?

LES: The first one was during the Korean War and was not actually at Christmas time. It was, let's see, I think we left in October and came back in November. We were gone 35 days all together. We flew first to Hawaii. In those days we didn't have jets. We were in propeller planes and flew to Hawaii. We did shows there at the Marine base, the Navy base and the Army base. Did four days there, then went on to Johnson Island, and then we island-hopped until we got to Okinawa. Did about three days in Okinawa at different bases and then went on to Japan and did some bases there. Then we spent two weeks in Korea. When we got there it was cold. We had parkas and everything. We even did a show in Pyongyang because when we got there we owned the whole peninsula. We had driven the North Koreans back to the Yalu River. The night after we left, the Chinese came across the Yalu River. I got the news when we were staying at the Imperial Hotel in Tokyo and called Bob and told him, "Hey, the Chinese have come across." He said, "You're kidding!" I said, "No, I'm not kidding, Bob, that's not a joking matter."

LES: You must have picked up a lot of new fans, permanent fans at that time. Do you still hear from those guys?

LES: Practically every place we play now, somebody will come up and say, "I saw you in Vinh Long, I saw you in Korat in Thailand or I saw you in Okinawa, I saw you there," and they reminisce about it and thank us. They want to thank us for being there and comin' over and making their life a little more cheerful. Vietnam, of course, was awful. It should never have happened, but it happened.

FRED: And you were there, you were in Vietnam?

LES: Oh yeah! We went to Vietnam eight years in a row from the time that silly Johnson sent people over there until it finally came to a stalemate around '72 or '73.

FRED: And now 17 years later as you and I talk, the band is still playing, probably often, for some of those same guys you played for overseas. Columbia Records has finally gotten around to reissuing a lot of the best things that the Les Brown Band of Renown ever did and this time they're in CD form, a beautiful sound all cleaned up and some things that haven't been available for a long while. For example, a fine recording of *All Through The Day* with Doris Day to sing and some exceptional trumpet playing right at the beginning. Who's that?

LES: It was probably Randy Brooks.

FRED: Randy was with you during what period of time?

LES: Oh, practically all during the war. He was 4-F. I was lucky to get him. He was one of the great trumpet players in the country and was 4-F. He had somethin' wrong that they wouldn't take him. I don't know why. So, during the war when you could find a good 4-F musician you latched onto 'em, over-paid 'em. He was a funny guy.

FRED: What kept you out of the war, Les?

LES: My children! Timing and my age. Every time they brought the age limit up to 40 I was called up again and something good would happen in Europe and they'd push it back to 35 and I was 36 or 37 with two children. But I made up for it I think. During the war, my God, we did an awful lot of one nighters and we played the Palladium and all the big places, Meadowbrook, Cafe Rouge in the Pennsylvania Hotel in New York and at least twice a week, and sometimes three, we'd go out and play a camp someplace where soldiers. . . Did a free concert for 'em.

FRED: Somewhere relatively nearby.

LES: Any place, really. Sometimes when we were on one-nighters we'd stop at an installation and do our concert and then go on to where we were playing that night.

FRED: That must have been wearying.

LES: In fact, that more or less helped me. I remember one guy on the draft board telling my manager (I never did get to the draft board), saying, "I think he's doing more good where he is than he would be in the Army."

FRED: Yeah, that's probably very true.

LES: Well, I was glad he said it and maybe that helped.

FRED: How did you happen to choose an old Irving Berlin tune *I've Got My Love To Keep Me Warm*, which became an enormous hit for you. Why that tune?

LES: When I was in college I saw the Dick Powell movie that was in and I loved the tune. I made an arrangement for the Duke Blue Devils and we used to play it in college. So, when we got with Columbia Records in the '40s I finally saw Skip Martin, who was doing a lot of arranging for us here in California, and I suggested the tune to him and he did it. That's quite a story, too, you know. We took it along as an extra to a recording date in 1945. If we had time, we'd do it. We had three to get in and we had 20 minutes left after we finished the first three so we made three shots at *Got My Love* and that was the last we heard of it for a long time until we played it on a Hope show in 1948. I got a call from New York saying, "Go in and record that right away." And, I says, "Fellows, if you'll look we recorded that **three years**

ago. Why don't you look for it?" They called back the next day, "We found it. We're going to put it out right away."

Otherwise, if they hadn't been listening that night it would still be at the bottom of the barrel where a lot of other things are. We must have at least 30 selections, if not more, at Columbia that have never been released, as any other band has. In fact, they have been going into things like that. For instance, on this new album, *On The Beach At Waikiki*, that was never released when it was first done. This is the first time I heard it since we recorded it.

FRED: Who were the soloists on *I've Got My Love To Keep Me Warm*, sax, piano, trumpet?

LES: Well, there was, in the order in which they appeared, Ted Nash on tenor sax, Geoff Clarkson on the piano, and Jimmy Zito on the trumpet.

FRED: So many tenor solos for so long were taken by Ted Nash with your band.

LES: Gosh, he played so beautifully. You know, he's sold all his instruments and has retired up to Carmel. He's up there with Doris. His wife was Doris's stand-in. All during her movie career they were close friends. Ted Nash and Eve, his wife, are living up in Carmel and they see Doris all the time and they are still the best of friends.

FRED: *Bizet Has His Day*. Whose concept was that and how did it happen to be recorded?

LES: Ben Homer. We were very lucky to have found Ben Homer at that one stage in our development. It was before we made a penny, by the way, in 1939. He was just out of Boston Conservatory and a very talented man but one of the laziest men that ever lived. I was lucky to get one arrangement every two months out of him.

FRED: That was his sole job, he didn't play with the band?

LES: No, he didn't play with the band. I don't know if he played any instrument. If anything, he played a little piano but not well enough to play with an orchestra. But he certainly could arrange. He was a wonderful arranger. The reason we did *Bizet Has His Day* was because in those days we couldn't go on the air and play any ASCAP tunes, you remember. We couldn't play anything but BMI tunes or Public Domain tunes so we had to make 'em up and that's why we recorded *Marche Slav*, *Mexican Hat Dance* and *Bizet Has His Day*. We even did *Old Dog Tray* by Stephen Foster and *Beautiful Dreamer*. We had to do anything to play, if we wanted to be on the air. If you weren't on the air, you weren't anywhere.

FRED: That's a particularly exciting treatment though. Was the clapping a spontaneous thing?

LES: I added that to give it a little verve, and I explained it to the people when we played. If they wanted to clap along, to think of the *Surrey With The Fringe On Top*, "bomp bomp a bomp bomp a bomp bomp a bomp bomp a bomp ah, etc." (Les beats out the tune). You know.

FRED: Sure, and there is a wonderful climax in the record in which the whole band shouts. I never did quite catch what it is they shout.

LES: "Yay!" That's all!

FRED: It's just, "Yay!" Was that your idea or did that just happen?

LES: That happened on the bandstand one night and I just said, "leave it in."

FRED: In the Columbia CD collection there is also *'Tis Autumn* which was an early hit for you and hasn't been heard from since then. Who was the vocalist?

LES: Oh, Ralph Young of Sandler and Young.

FRED: Oh, is that so?

LES: That's my arrangement, by the way, *'Tis Autumn*.

FRED: You playing alto on that?

149

Les Brown

LES: No, I just arranged it. Just recently, we were honored by the Big Band Academy here in town and we played a retrospective of our records. Had the whole band in. I had Ralph come up and sing *'Tis Autumn* with the band. Now we've lost the old arrangement. We have no idea where it is, so I had to make another arrangement for him in a different key because he now sings about a tone lower than he did when he was younger.

FRED: Also in the CD is Lucy Ann Polk singing Frank Comstock's arrangement of *S'Wonderful*. That is another absolute triumph. That record is the greatest opener of all time. I cannot tell you how many radio shows I've opened that with. It includes a very exciting trumpet solo by, I presume, Don Fagerquist.

LES: If it was good trumpet, it was Fagerquist because he was the greatest I've ever had.

FRED: Yeah, he was with you for quite a long time, wasn't he, Les?

LES: Yeah.

FRED: A good choice in Doris Day's songs was *My Dreams Are Getting Better All The Time*. There's a funny little doubling of the tempo underneath her vocal, just quickly, and then out and then later it picks up again.

LES: Yeah, that's my arrangement.

FRED: Is it? You're to be congratulated.

LES: Thank you. I don't know, I thought the tune was a little dull (LES does a little verbal beat by singing) like a schotische, so I thought, (LES does another little verbal beat) it would be a little better for our style so I just doubled up the tempo after she sang and then kept it going that way and when she came back in and then slowed up at the end. I imagine if anybody tried to dance to it they'd stumble around a little!

FRED: And on *We'll Be Together Again* you do a verse which I'd never heard.

LES: It's a beautiful Frank Comstock arrangement and a great tune.

FRED: That's written by Carl Fisher and Frankie Laine, I think.

LES: Right. I published the tune too.

FRED: I didn't know you had your own publishing firm.

LES: I started one because of that tune and put my brother, Warren, in charge of it. He went to New York and even though the tune didn't become a big hit at the time, it's now considered a standard. It got him started in the publishing business and he finally ended up with Leeds Music which was bought by MCA. My brother, Warren, is now retired. He was very successful as the head of MCA Music after they bought Leeds, and he worked at Universal out here for over 20 years.

FRED: And on the CD is a record I used to play a lot when I had a radio station in Gallup, New Mexico, right after World War II. Way out in the middle of nowhere we used to play *There's Good Blues Tonight*.

LES: Yeah, that's written by my good friend Glenn Osser. He wrote the tune and his wife wrote the lyrics, or they wrote them together or something.

FRED: What a great conductor and arranger he is.

LES: Yeah, well, he is a very good friend of mine. Like George Shearing, when they are in town, they always stay with me. He wrote the tune and Gabriel Heatter, I guess it was, used to come on the air on the radio saying, "Ah, there's good news tonight."

FRED: Oh, yes.

LES: I don't know why because I don't think there ever was any good news any time.

FRED: No, especially not during that period of time.

LES: Or now!

FRED: Or now, yeah. Was there any particular band that you thought was the best you ever had?

LES: By far the best I ever had was in the early '50s when I had Ronnie Lang on first sax. He played some wonderful alto solos, and Dave Pell on tenor. We had Abe Most on clarinet, Don Fagerquist on trumpet, Wes Hensel on trumpet, and Don Paladino on first trumpet. Fagerquist played some wonderful things. Tony Rizzi was on guitar, Jack Sperling at the drums, Geoff Clarkson at the piano, and Dick Noel on trombone. Ray Sims was a wonderful trombone soloist. Stumpy was on bass trombone. Butch Stone of course was on baritone. What a band! That's the band that made that *Concert At the Palladium* album which is the best thing we ever did, and it was taken off the air.

FRED: Yeah, those were wonderful—two albums—four sides all together and came out on Coral Records. Some things were on there that were not anywhere else, *Crazy Legs*, for example.

LES: Frank Comstock wrote that. The solos are just tremendous.

FRED: Everything! It crackles, the band just sounds inspired, Les.

LES: It was Sonny Burke's idea. We were with Coral Records at the time and he was my closest friend. We used to have our martinis together practically every night. We were booked to go into the Palladium I think for five weeks, so every night we were on twice a night for some reason or other. Radio was still fairly big and we recorded everything we did. Of course, Sonny Burke made sure we had a good balance. He talked to the engineer and helped place the mikes and everything. He was very good. He did an awful lot of Sinatra's albums.

FRED: Have you had to do a lot of the nitty gritty work in managing right along or in recent years have others done that for you?

LES: I was always the policy maker and everything. I didn't bother with the actual booking. I had Don Kramer who was my drummer and roommate my senior year at Duke University. He joined the band when my brother, Warren, who was managing the band, went into the Navy. Then I brought in Don Kramer as manager of the band. Then when we got to California, he did all the booking, too.

FRED: Who's doing it now?

LES: This was after we had spent our seven years with MCA and we went back to Consolidated Radio Artists. This was after, what would you say, we became independent.

FRED: And you've been independent ever since.

LES: Yes.

FRED: Who's managing the band right now on a day to day basis?

LES: My brother, Stumpy.

FRED: Finding a good sideman seems to be no problem for you. You have real stability there.

LES: Oh, we have an organized band, and the reason I keep the same men is because we don't travel. We stay in California. There is an occasional trip—we just finished a four-day trip that included three in North Carolina because I was celebrating my 50 years of "banding" and we wanted to do it at Duke University where it started. I started the endowment for a Chair there, The Les Brown Endowment For a Chair In Music at Duke University, which we hope will come to fruition in the next four or five years. We did a benefit concert there with George Shearing, by the way, and then we went to Dallas on the way back. That was our only tour of the year.

FRED: Actually you are pretty busy out here, aren't you, busy as you want to be?

LES: Busy as I want to be. We do about 120 gigs a year, which comes to a little over two a week. But we're a dance band and most of our work, Fred, is for private parties. I don't think we are open to the public more than 5% of our engagements a year.

The only time—now and then we do a concert—we're doing one down at Performing Arts in Orange County next month. I guess it's with Patti Page. That's open to the public. We've done that sort of thing with Mel Torme and others like Frankie Laine over at Pasadena and we do a weekend for Disneyland. All the rest are private parties. You can't get in unless you're invited. People say "Where are you playing next?" and I say, "I don't know." It's mostly affluent parties and people that grew up with us who now can afford these. They go anywhere from $500 a person to $5,000 a person.

FRED: Wow! Probably black-tie.

LES: Oh, practically all. We wear more tuxedos than we do our uniforms. We have two uniforms plus the tuxedos and when there is a black-tie party we have to wear tuxedos and they want us to. The band looks good in them too. Even better, when you mingle with the guests. Then they don't know the difference except by their age. The age group for the parties we play for are definitely over 50— the 60s and 70s.

FRED: You still start your opening set with *Leap Frog*?

LES: No, no, if I started out that high at one of these parties we'd never be asked back. That comes at the end of the evening, after the dinner. Most of them are dinner dances and we have what is known as a dinner-set. Frankly I can't stand loud music when I'm eating.

FRED: No, neither can I.

LES: And we hold it way down until they have had enough to drink and they've finished the dinner and their speeches and then we go all out.

FRED: Where did *Leap Frog* come from?

LES: *Leap Frog* was written by the same gentleman who wrote *In The Mood*. His name was Joe Garland and he was a tenor saxophone player with Louis Armstrong. We carried that around with us on the road for at least nine months before we got around to trying it. As soon as we did we decided to make it our theme. Come on the air jumping instead of a pretty thing we had used before. When we came to the Palladium in 1942 for the first time ever, we were doing a movie and playing the Palladium at night. Boy, it was tired-time! We started using *Leap Frog* then as our theme.

FRED: As you and I talk here in late 1990, you have a new album that is about to appear on the USA label.

LES: We did an album for Duke University. I started a Chair down at Duke University and put in X-amount of dollars and other friends have and we made this album. It was mostly ballads, easy stuff. We did a lot of bass flutes, alto flutes. We added a harp at one time. We added a couple of French horns for one date and we used a lot of the old sound with the four trumpet mutes and the four trombones and the guitar an octave lower. Frank Comstock did most of the arrangements. Frank Comstock and Jay Hill. This was all done at the behest of a Duke alumnus who was a friend of mine and he bankrolled the thing. He said, "We'll get this and we'll send it out to all the Duke Alumni and I'll get different kinds of mailing lists and all that." He did and it raised, oh, over $100,000 that way. People just contributed to the Les Brown Band. So, what we did then, we went back in and did some jazz things. We did *Love For Sale*, *Anything Goes*, and all the royalties are going to the Les Brown Fund at Duke University to establish a Chair in music down there. We have ten years to do it and I hope to get it done while I'm still here.

FRED: You know, it seems to me you have had a very satisfying life and are still living it today. In general you must be pleased with the way things have gone for you.

LES: Oh, I consider myself lucky. I was at the right place at the right time a couple of times, especially when we got the Bob Hope Show. Without that I think we would have gone the way of all other bands. There's not that much demand for big bands anymore but with my television work and radio work and so many years of it, and then I'd saved a little money and made some good and bad investments, mostly good or a little better than the bad ones. I don't have to work, but I still enjoy it and as long as I have my health I'm going to!

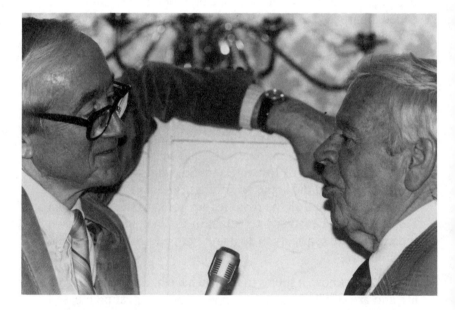

LES BROWN and the Author in 1989. (Ray Avery photo)

9

THE TWO HELENS

Big Band singers began and often remained performers with a secondary status. They were not, as a rule, truly musicians and they spent most of their time sitting on the edge of the bandstand crossing their legs and, in the case of the girls, tossing their curly locks in tempo with the music. They were usually paid no better than the sidemen and received recording fees of as little as $15.00 a side or, as Ray Eberle once told me, "Two for $25.00." Some few developed such distinctive styles that they found themselves with fan clubs and legions of admirers who would cluster about the bandstands to cheer them on. Bing Crosby was the first to break loose as a star in his own right. Much later came Frank Sinatra, Dick Haymes, Perry Como, Peggy Lee, Bea Wain, Ella Mae Morse, Kitty Kallen and others. Few were "superstars" while remaining part of the team.

Among the "girls," as they were called, two were universally acclaimed. They were Helen Forrest and Helen O'Connell. Helen O'Connell, partnered with Bob Eberly (Ray's older brother) was responsible for hit after hit for the Jimmy Dorsey band. Helen Forrest was the vocal star of **three** of the biggest bands, Artie Shaw, Benny Goodman and Harry James. Both

Helens went on to develop successful solo careers themselves. As this was being written, both were still singing and performing but their approaches to music, show business and life in general couldn't have been more different. Let's consider Helen Forrest first, interviewed initially at a concert in the late '70s.

Helen Forrest

FRED: Before Artie Shaw, where were you?

HELEN: In radio.

FRED: Were you in New York?

HELEN: I started on WNEW in New York City. I was doing all kinds of little commercial things, spot commercials. I was called Marlene, Helene—anything that rhymed with Helene or Helen. I stayed on WNEW for about a year and then I went to CBS. There were music-pluggers in those days. Remember?

FRED: Sure.

HELEN: And of course I got very close to all of them and they told Mark Warnow about me. He is no longer living. He had a program called the Blue Velvet Hour. I auditioned for him and he said "Yes, you would be great." But what he did, he called them the Blue Velvet Musicians. The Blue Velvet Hour with Bonnie Blue. I was Bonnie Blue. You remember it? Really?

FRED: I remember it was the name you had used. Yes, of course.

HELEN: But he wouldn't let anybody know who I was. He said, "You are going to be the mystery lady." And I said, "But, Mark, that is ridiculous." So for one year I was Bonnie Blue and nobody knew who I was. He would make me come in the back door and go out the back door. It **was** ridiculous, but it was a great show. Fantastic show.

FRED: How did you get involved with Shaw.

HELEN: Well, from there I went to Washington, D.C. My brother moved to Washington and the whole family went. There was a job open for a singer in a Spanish American restaurant which was **the** place to eat for all the politicians, the congressmen. I went in for two weeks and I stayed for two years. While I was there Ziggy Elman told Artie and he told Benny about me. Well, Artie came in to hear me and offered me a job. But I didn't go. I was going with the drummer, so I stayed. Benny came in to hear me and he said, "Whoever said she could sing?" and turned around and walked out. That was just Benny's way. But Artie told me, "When you're ready to leave, send me a wire and a demonstration record, that's all." He was working in Baltimore on a one-nighter, and I had just about had it after two years, so I sent him a telegram which said "I'm ready." I sent him the record. He said, "Meet us in New York." And that was it, I joined him.

FRED: There was a period when you and Billie Holiday were both singing with Artie Shaw.

HELEN: Yes, Billie would sit on one side and I would sit on the other and it was fantastic. Of course, Billie would get very angry with Artie because he wouldn't let her sing. He said he didn't have any arrangements for her. I said, "Well, give her mine."

FRED: Did you find her someone from whom you could learn?

HELEN: Oh, yes, she was a beautiful person. Absolutely fantastic! I didn't really get into Billie's singing because that was not my style. Billie was more blues and I was strictly ballad in those days.

FRED: Who among the early singers did you admire? Mildred Bailey? Who?

HELEN: Yes, you just hit it and of course the queen, Ella Fitzgerald. I think Ella was my complete favorite.

FRED: It seems to me that your first record with the Shaw band was something like *You're A Sweet Little Headache*.

HELEN: Oh, no, you're right!

FRED: The first hit was *Deep In A Dream*?

HELEN: Yes, you're right! Oh, I haven't thought of that in years.

FRED: You mean you don't get requests for those things **nowadays?**

HELEN: No, in fact, they don't ask for anything with Artie.

FRED: Not even *Deep Purple*?

HELEN: No. Once in a while. Then I know that's a true fan.

FRED: You were with Shaw for what, a couple of years?

HELEN: Right. Two years.

FRED: Did you leave at the time that Artie retired and the band broke up?

HELEN: The minute Artie broke up the band, I left and I kind of pouted. I didn't know which way I wanted to go, and then I joined Benny Goodman.

FRED: Benny, I've always heard can be a terribly difficult man to work for.

HELEN: Yes, I stayed with Benny for two years. He was a great task-master. He was a perfectionist, but that's what made him the great clarinetist that he was. He was truly very hard to get along with. The only two things that I did with Benny that I really liked were *More Than You Know* and *The Man I Love*.

FRED: You were with Benny, and then went directly to James?

HELEN: No, I wouldn't say directly. Maybe I was off a month or something. In those days you went directly. If you didn't have a job every week, everybody dies... Well, I guess I took a month or so off and then I heard that Harry (James) was auditioning singers, and at that time Harry had Dick Haymes with him. He wanted a "jump" singer, he didn't want a ballad singer. When I went to audition for him, he said, "I know your work, Helen, and it's not because you're not a great singer and I really think you are great, but I really want a jazz singer." He said, "Dick Haymes is doing all the ballads and I need a jazz singer." I said, "O.K.

just let me audition." He had strings then, so I said, "I'll make a deal with you. If the boys in the band vote me in, do I have the job?" He knew he was dead because I knew every boy, every musician in the whole group. I'd already worked with them. He had a brand new arrangement of *But Not For Me* and I sang it. He cued me in and it was a gorgeous thing. Of course, the band applauded. They all stood up and he said, "Well, it looks like you're in." He didn't really fight too hard.

FRED: That's my favorite record that you did with the band.

HELEN: Really?

FRED: Really. I loved *Skylark* and so many of the others. I suppose I get more requests for *I Don't Want To Walk Without You* than anything.

HELEN: That one, I get requests for that one and *I Had The Craziest Dream*. They are not too familiar with *But Not For Me*.

FRED: Of the three bands, which one was the most fun to work with?

HELEN: No question, Harry! When I went with Harry, he said, "Helen, I can't afford you. I can't pay you. I know what you were making. You were making top money as a band vocalist when you left Benny." I said, "I don't care what you pay. There's only one thing that I want. I want to start a chorus and I want to finish it. Don't start—I don't want the band chorus—don't put me in the middle and then have me sit down." And that's what he did—that's why these songs became so famous.

FRED: He tailored things for you.

HELEN: Right! He made them for the singer, instead of all instrumental.

FRED: Did *I Cried For You* evolve or was it the first time you did it, what it turned out to be? There was **so much** emotional appeal in that record.

HELEN: Well, the thing that I loved about Harry—he didn't just get the song and then walk into the recording studio and do it. We would play it on the bandstand for at least a month, maybe two months and then we would record it.

FRED: You got into some pictures with him. I recall one, it seems to me, with somebody like Cesar Romero and what was it *Springtime in the Rockies*?

HELEN: Right, with Betty Grable.

FRED: Betty Grable, of course, that's where they met.

HELEN: *I Had The Craziest Dream*, that's right.

FRED: And did you do some other pictures, too?

HELEN: Yes. We did *Two Girls and A Sailor*. I did *I Cried For You* in that.

FRED: Did you make a lot of money in those days, working with those bands or did you not? I talked to Martha Tilton once and she said, "You know, really it was mostly for kicks because we didn't make that much."

HELEN: Actually I disagree. When you say "make a lot of money", in those days—**yes**.

FRED: Seventy-five dollars a week was a lot of money?

HELEN: Exactly,because the work packages the way they are today and everything, you could buy a Coke for nickel.

FRED: You could have a meal for a dime.

HELEN: Exactly. So actually when I left Harry I was making something between $400 and $500 a week which was a fortune. So I was the top paid vocalist in the country. Now let's face it, that was a lot of money. But in those days it came too easy, we threw it away.

FRED: Well now, how was it touring with all of these guys with the band—on a bus all of the time?

HELEN: Fantastic. I was never so protected in my life. In fact they used to shoo them away. I'd say, "I'm only **talking** to the

HELEN FORREST, taken shortly after she left the Harry James band for a solo career. (Ray Avery photo)

man." I was so protected, they wouldn't let anybody within twenty feet of me. I was the baby, you couldn't get near me.

FRED: After the war, singers began to take over from bands and I remember listening to you every week with Dick Haymes and Gordon (Gordy) Jenkins on the Autolite radio show.

HELEN: Three years—right, with Dick Haymes. Oh, what a fabulous show that was. Gordy would write a new vignette and every week we had something brand new. Fantastic, the greatest show. And of course, my first love is radio—I'm sorry, I love it.

FRED: Of all of the things you've recorded with Shaw and Goodman and James and on your own - can you pick out a few that are your personal favorites, whether or not they were hits?

HELEN: Yes, I can name them real fast. *I Had The Craziest Dream, I Don't Want To Walk Without You, I Cried For You, But Not For Me, It Seems To Me I've Heard That Song Before*, right down the line. I love every one of them, they all have a message for me, that's why.

FRED: You know, my favorite record you did with Shaw is a thing called *I'm In Love With The Honorable Mr. So-and-So.*

HELEN: I love that song, I love it.

FRED: Sam Coslow. One of those tunes that was from a Walter Pidgeon movie, *Society Lawyer*, or something like that.

HELEN: You're right. Yes, that was a gorgeous song.

FRED: And I don't think it ever really got anywhere.

HELEN: You know, it's funny, I have an album—a medley that was written for me by Gordon Jenkins and I do the story of my professional life with Artie, with Benny, with Harry. When I first started doing it originally, I'd do about eight bars of the song— each song that I did with the band. I was doing *I'm In Love With The Honorable Mr. So-and-So*—well, nobody knew the song so I had to take it out and I finally wound up doing *All The Things You Are.*

FRED: Did you—from the time you left James—work as a single?

HELEN: Oh, yes.

FRED: And you are still doing that today.

HELEN: Still am.

FRED: Ever get tired of it?

HELEN: I get tired of traveling and packing—the four walls of the hotel, but I never get tired of singing.

FRED: Did you try retiring from the business at any time?

HELEN: No, never—never. No, I stayed out for a few months to have my son and that was it. You know I thought about retiring and I'd think, "Oh, I can't stop singing. That's ridiculous."

AUTHOR'S NOTE: In mid-summer of 1990, I talked with Helen via telephone. She had undergone quite serious surgery and had been inactive for many long months. As we spoke, she was planning a couple of trial engagements to test her endurance and bookings had been made. Her own 1982 book, *I Had the Craziest Dream*, published by Putnam, was out of print but is well worth a hunt in your public library. She had made a new album, "Now and Forever" on Stash Records which showed that she remained a superb stylist and gave her a chance to stretch out with musicians such as Hank Jones and Frank Wess. Living in the San Fernando Valley, she had, until her illness, been constantly on tour with stage presentations put together with long-time manager Joe Graydon. She told me her friends and fans were giving her constant support and encouragement, that she was looking forward to her grown son moving from Phoenix to Los Angeles, and most of all, looking forward to getting back to work.

Helen O'Connell

Helen O'Connell, too, had maintained a successful career in clubs, theaters, on records and on television, where she had once served as co-host on the "Today" show. Looking half her age, still pert and blonde and dynamic, she had toured with the "Four Girls Four" (with Kay Starr, Rosemary Clooney and Rose Marie) and sung from time to time with the Jimmy Dorsey band, led by trumpeter Lee Castle. I had been the host for such an occasion at the Hyatt Regency O'Hare in Chicago for my then Windy City affiliate, WAIT. Nearly five hundred customers from five states had to be turned away when the ballroom reached capacity. Such was her draw. But, surprisingly, music had never been the motivating force in her life. The interviews were done in 1983 and 1991.

HELEN: Well, I worked for my living and some parts of it I liked very much. I guess in my case I would say I've lived for my children and I don't mean that as a pat on the back to me, its just been my life and that's my main interest.

FRED: You have three grown daughters, do you?

HELEN: Four.

FRED: Four, is that so? Any of them in show business?

HELEN: No, not a one. Never really leaned that way, actually. They had some opportunities, and they just weren't interested, really. I have four grown daughters and six grandchildren.

FRED: I cannot believe this grandmother bit.

HELEN: Listen, my oldest grandson is more than twenty-five years old, so I could be a great grandmother, "even as I speak," as they say.

FRED: You joined the Jimmy Dorsey band in 1938 and the first record I remember hearing and falling in love with by you with Jimmy Dorsey was *One Sweet Letter From You*. It was recorded in August of 1939. Listening to you perform today in person or on television, on one of those PBS shows, it's amazing that your style is exactly the same as it was. It appears that you arrived on scene with your style full-blown and developed.

HELEN: I have always sung the same way. It's the only way I know to sing. I've been asked questions about my style before. In the beginning, which was a long time ago, I didn't know what anybody was talking about. I didn't know what they meant. I couldn't answer their questions because I didn't know what the question was, really. They said, "Where did you get your style?" and I said, "What style? I don't know. It's just the same way I talk, the only way I've ever sung."

FRED: I know you broke into show business in Toledo, Ohio. How did you get involved in—I think you were with the Larry Funk Band—before Jimmy Dorsey? How did you get from Toledo to New York City where you first got involved with his band?

HELEN: I left Toledo with a small band from Ohio and stayed with them over a year and a half. Jimmy Richards was a very good nine-piece band. They were fine musicians and it was just terrific that I had a chance to work with good people and good musicians. After that, I went to St. Louis and had—it wasn't really my own radio show—but I was featured on it at KSD with Russ David, who is a fine pianist, arranger, everything. He still is very active in St. Louis music. I did that for several months and my sister, who sings (doesn't sing anymore) but was singing then, and her husband had a group playing at the Chase Hotel in the Steeplechase Lounge. They were there, I think, over two years. Larry Funk's Band was playing in the main dining room of the same hotel. I'd go in and see my sister and once in a while her husband would get me to sing a song.

Larry Funk heard me there and wanted me to go on the road with him. I didn't want to. I wanted to stay where I was doing radio work. I loved it, not traveling and being sort of, more or less "settled," in a single room in a boarding house. That was settled to me. My sister told him that I would take the job and

167

then came and told me that she had accepted for me. I said, "How can you do that?" She said, "I did, so you'll have to go." I was **really** upset about it, not that I didn't like Larry Funk or his band, they were marvelous, but I didn't want to leave and travel again. She said, "No, you have to go, because it's better for you. You'll never get anyplace here," blah, blah, blah——so off I went and that's how I got to New York.

FRED: Jimmy Dorsey actually heard you himself or was it his secretary?

HELEN: Two different people that I know of, his secretary and a friend of hers, who was at that time at Harvard, and also wrote a column on music, Mike Levin, I think also the fellow that became my manager later, Semour Heller. At any rate, I think it was Nita (Moore) and Mike who first spoke to Jimmy about me, because he was looking for a singer and said, "Why don't you go down and hear her?" Because, of course, there was no TV then.

FRED: You weren't doing any live radio shots at. . .

HELEN: Yes, we were. That's how they heard me. They heard me on the radio from The Village Bar. They said, "Why don't you go down and see her and see how she looks. See if she looks as good as she sounds." So they came down to see how I looked. They sent Mr. Burton, the manager of Jimmy Dorsey's Band. It was a couple of days later when they hired me. I'll never forget the way they hired me. He said, "I guess you got the job. We've never had a girl singer yet who didn't have fat legs." I think we all had——sort of—teenage fat.

We all started very young, you know. I know when I got out of Ohio and found I had an extra 15 cents or something I would have a chocolate or strawberry sundae with my breakfast. I went up to 145 pounds one time. That was my top weight except when I was pregnant. But it was just teenage fat and when I lost a job with an orchestra that I had auditioned for, I took the weight off. In one month I lost 26 pounds and I never put it back on and I'm not going to, God willing.

HELEN O'CONNELL in publicity shot of about 1950. She looked
almost the same in 1991. (Ray Avery photo)

FRED: I believe that. I hear Jimmy Dorsey was an absolute pussy cat, one of the nicest people on the music scene.

HELEN: We had a rather unique group, in that respect. I think if anybody came into the band and didn't get along well or was a troublemaker, I don't care how well he played, he didn't stay there very long. Jimmy was just a wonderful person to work with and work for. It was more like working **with** him. He never was the boss.

FRED: In the very beginning you seemed to be assigned mostly novelty and up tunes and no ballads.

HELEN: No, I didn't do any ballads because Bob Eberly did them all and he really couldn't handle an up-tempo tune. He didn't care to and really didn't sound too good on it, although he would try it once in a while. We both did novelty tunes together, but he did most of the ballads and I did the things with a beat.

FRED: You were on the move quite a lot with the band at that time, I guess. On the road constantly?

HELEN: Yes, pretty much so. I think I had two vacations in four years, one was for ten days and one was for two weeks.

FRED: Tell me about Bob Eberly. I've always understood he was a great pleasure to work with.

HELEN: That's an understatement. If you didn't know him you wouldn't know that, but only the highest praise could be good enough for Bob. He was just a super, super person, human-being. Everybody in the band, **everybody** looked up to him and enjoyed his company and laughed at him. He had a great wit and he was just a good friend and a good person.

FRED: One time Dick Haymes told me that Bob was his idea of a great singer.

HELEN: Oh, yes, he used to come in and listen to Bob every chance he got. If we were in New York and Dick was in New York, he would just sit and listen and listen and listen, with his mother Marguerite Haymes. Nobody could capture Bob's feeling with a song, nobody.

FRED: It became a trademark that with the Jimmy Dorsey Band there would be many performances where Bob would sing a song as a ballad, then the tempo would double and you'd sing it up and swinging in contrasting rhythm. Was that an innovation of the arranger, Tutti Camarata?

HELEN: We were doing a radio show and it had many elements of a happy birthday thing and calling somebody on the phone. I'd do all kinds of gimmicks in it so that the half hour show went by very quickly. But there wasn't time for Jimmy and Bob and me to each do a song. So Tutti Camarata got the idea of putting us all on the same song, but in our own way, you know, in different tempos. So because of necessity that idea was born.

FRED: Did the record company, Decca in this case, want to record something like that? It seems to me I've heard that the Kapp Brothers thought that it wouldn't sell because people wouldn't want to dance to the varying tempos.

HELEN: I don't know if they thought it wouldn't sell. They thought it wouldn't go well in jukeboxes because of people dancing to jukebox music then. I certainly can see their point, but as it turned out, people loved it and it went very well in jukeboxes and everyplace else.

FRED: And it's still going well, in jukeboxes—the few of them that are still around.

HELEN: Yes I know, I've seen the records in jukeboxes.

FRED: Did you have a hit right away or did it take several recordings before that particular concept caught on?

HELEN: Oh that concept, the first one caught on. I think the first one was *Amapola*. Bob always said it was and I'm sure he knew.

FRED: I'm getting ahead of myself. How about when you first joined Jimmy? At that point were there hit records for you with the band?

HELEN: Yes, I think the first one I did was my second recording with him, that really made any noise. That arrangement was written specifically for me. The first recording I did was written for the girl who had been there before, Ella Mae Morse. She left and I replaced her and I did that arrangement and I liked it. It was called *Romance Runs In the Family*. Then the second one that I did was one written—the arrangement was written for me—which was *All Of Me*. That was the hit and it's always been a hit for me. So my first one that was done for me was a hit.

FRED: And that stayed very much in all of the MCA collections.

HELEN: I've been identified with it quite a bit ever since then.

FRED: Great tune! Also, obviously a superb recording of *Embraceable You*.

HELEN: That was the big hit for me, too. I had quite a few singles—I don't think as many as Bob, but I had a lot of silly novelty tunes. Some were fun and some weren't. Some were pretty successful, *Arthur Murray Taught Me Dancing In a Hurry* and *Six Lessons From Madam Lazonga* and things like that were pretty successful. But they are not really what you hunt for when you want to really sing a song, get your teeth into it. They are fun things.

FRED: Johnny Mercer did one of those two, didn't he?

HELEN: He did *Arthur Murray*. . .because that was from the movie *The Fleet's In*, the same as *Tangerine*, the same as *Build a Better Mousetrap*, *Not Mine* and all those marvelous things that he did.

FRED: I remember seeing you in the picture. Then there was another one with Red Skelton wasn't there?

HELEN: Yes, it was called *I Dood It* and the only song from that that we were associated with was *Star Eyes*, but I left Jimmy before he recorded that number, although I've been associated with it always. When I came back in the business after seven years of being away I recorded *Star Eyes* for Capital. I still was associated with it, even though I didn't make the record, because of the movie.

FRED: Kitty Kallen did the record. . .?

HELEN: Yes, I'm sure she did.

FRED: You and Kitty were, I think, quite different sounding but it's funny how well she worked out with the Jimmy Dorsey Band.

HELEN: Yes, she's just a darling. I saw her just a few weeks ago. She looks great and she sounds good, but, she says, she's afraid to go on stage.

FRED: I think your most celebrated recording, far and away, is *Green Eyes* and the way you handled the lyrics, "cool and limpid green eyes." How did that come about?

HELEN: Well, first of all, most of our recordings were made the next day after we first heard a song. We'd start at 2:00 o'clock at the Cafe Rouge and rehearse. Quite often we'd go in the next day and record them. I didn't even know them. As I can't read music I was really hunting for notes. But on that particular song we rehearsed because it was the only time Jimmy was trying to tell me how to sing something. The reason he was telling me was because my range wasn't quite high enough or big enough to go from the low E flat which is the bottom note up to the notes that sit up high on those particular words; "cool and limpid." So he got the clarinet and he was trying to tell me how to just touch the note and then I could hit them, if I did that, you know.

So the next day on the way to the Decca Studio, I was in the car with Nita Moore, the secretary who first told him about me. She said, "What are you recording today?" I said, "I don't know, I guess the thing we did last night." I never knew what I was going to record. She said, "That?" and I said "Yes, why?" She said, "You can't do that, that's too high for you." I said, "I know it but I guess I'll do it, I don't know." We all walked in and they pulled out the music and I did it that way.

FRED: An absolute total show stopper, still today.

HELEN: It was because I couldn't hit the note, that's all (laughter).

FRED: Of course, I have to ask you—do you get tired of doing that?

HELEN: No, not as long as people want to hear it. Why would I get tired of it? No, absolutely not. The reaction and the response is such that it would keep me from getting tired of that.

FRED: Obviously the kind of feedback you get from the audience keeps you young, keeps you feeling good about yourself. Am I right about that? Is that thing that comes back at you from out there very important?

HELEN: It's very reassuring and very flattering and it does make you feel good, yes.

FRED: How did you happen to leave the Jimmy Dorsey Band? For marriage?

HELEN: Yes, precisely. I wanted to get married and have children and that was my biggest aim in life, biggest goal. I wanted to devote all my time and attention to it because I didn't think I could do justice to it if I kept working. I didn't see how that could be possible, so I quit.

FRED: And in that period you were just staying home and having kids?

HELEN: That's right, and I loved it.

FRED: And then the Today Show came along.

HELEN: Oh, no. I went back to work quite a while before that. My husband left me and I had three mouths, at that time, to feed (four now) but I had to go to work. It's as simple as that. So I went back to work with Frank De Vol at the Palladium. Then Vic Damone took me on tour with him. He was very sweet to do that. Then I went on the road right from that tour for a year with Martin and Lewis—off and on, for a year. They are personal friends. Then I got into doing a single in nightclubs. I remember working so hard up in Elko, Nevada, to make myself raise my hands because a band singer never moved, you know. It was a whole new thing for me to even move a finger and to break in my arrangements I had had made for nightclub purposes. I worked around Elko and someplace in Tucson. Just trying to get an act in shape. Then I started doing a single.

FRED: How did you get involved with the Today Show?

HELEN: I just don't know.

FRED: Weren't you already doing some television?

HELEN: No, I don't think that had anything to do with it, really. Yes, Bob Eberly and I had done the Perry Como summer replacement. Bob and I had a summer show with Russ Morgan. The first time I did any acting, to speak of, was on NBC's Matinee Theater, which was an hour and a half or two hours, I've forgotten, and live.

FRED: Live?

HELEN: Yes, I did that with Craig Stevens. I had just done that, when the Today Show wanted me. I was promised some more of these to do, and I would like to have pursued that, but the Today Show was very tempting. So I went there.

FRED: That must have been an all-consuming life. You had to get up at, what, 3:00 in the morning or something?

HELEN: When I lived out in Long Island, I did because I never knew if it had snowed during the night and I'd slip and slide all the way into Manhattan by myself and it was still dark out. Until I got my apartment ready in New York, it was a question of transporting the three girls back and forth to Marymount School in New York and picking them up after school and getting myself to work. I remember going to bed before they even had their dinner at night. It was such a turnabout for me, although I'd been used to getting up early with children, I'd been back in show business for quite a while where you work nights. And so it was turning my life around again.

FRED: Was the show done then on the corner of Rockefeller Center where people could look in and you could look out?

HELEN: Expedition Hall, I think it was called, with the glass windows. We used to go out and do the man-on-the-street interviews.

FRED: I must say that television at that stage of the game must have been a lot of fun.

HELEN: It was. We had a good time on the Today Show. Dave (Garroway) and Frank (Blair) and Jack Lescoulie and I used to have a lot of good, good laughs, when we would do remotes out in the city, good times just talking or having dinner or having a drink, or laughing at the meetings after the show every day. It was a good group, it was fun.

FRED: Let me ask you briefly about a couple of the other hit records you did with Jimmy Dorsey. There was, of course, *Brazil*, and *Yours* and another tune that I always thought had the most insipid lyrics of all times but became a big hit, was *Jim*.

HELEN: Oh, I don't think it was so insipid.

FRED: How could any woman be in love with such a total rat?

HELEN: I think that a lot of women have been in love with a rat. I didn't think of Jim as a rat when I sang the song—not at all.

FRED: I think one of the best records was *When The Sun Comes Out*.

HELEN: Yes, it was one of the best tunes I ever got to sing. I'm glad it's a big record, too. I introduced that song. I was the first one to ever hear it, they said. They played it for me up at the old Brill Building. I was the first one to record it.

FRED: If you had anything to do differently, looking back, is there anything that you would have done dramatically differently than you did, in such a long and consistently successful career?

HELEN: I think I would have probably had to make the same decisions again because you have to follow your heart, and my heart was at home with my children and that's where I wanted to be. There were some things that I turned down that could have been very big opportunities—moving picture contracts. I turned down several offers from Paramount and MGM, but it was not what I wanted to do then. I wanted to be home with my babies. One came along later, an offer from Universal that I couldn't do because the offer wasn't as much money as I was making on the road at that time. I needed money desperately for my family at that time so had to turn it down.

FRED: You are very active as we talk, here in 1991, in the Society of Singers, a non-profit organisation created to provide help and understanding to professional singers. Some truly celebrated singers of the past have had tough times in the present. Sometimes that's been due to inept or unscrupulous management or record companies.

HELEN: Those singers just didn't think anyone would do those things to them. They were sort-of trusting souls. By-and-large I think people in show business don't have much sense about money. Their minds are filled with more creative things. They feel that if they have a friend he's a friend who is loyal and is going to take care of them. There were too many horror stories. More than there should have been.

FRED: Well, if you're a singer or care about people who sing you should certainly join the Society of Singers. We're talking right now at the national headquarters here at 8242 West Third Street, Suite 250, Los Angeles, California 90048. There are chapters in New York City, Las Vegas, and Chicago.

HELEN: Our aim is not just to help people or see that abuse doesn't happen again, but to help youngsters or anyone who's in the business now who needs advice. I'm sure if they join SOS they're entitled to put their plight in front of somebody or get advice from somebody here.

FRED: Well, people working together tend to work things out.

HELEN: Oh, sure! It's about time singers got together. I think they're always had a very close tie, somehow, this just puts it altogether.

FRED: And you're going to keep right on singing?

HELEN: I certainly am, until I get very wealthy and that will never happen (laughter).

10

HARRY JAMES

The Swing Era was brilliant but brief. In a span of ten, maybe fifteen years, the Kings of Swing climbed the heights and reigned supreme. But by the early 50s the glory times were gone. Only a handful survived. One of the most successful ever was Harry James. He outsold records, out-grossed at theaters and clubs and ballrooms and continued to pack 'em in until a week before he died, in 1983. Born in Albany, Georgia, while the Mighty Haag Circus was on tour, Harry was raised in Texas. Harry's middle name was Haag. His father, Everett, led the Number One Band and his mother performed in the circus as an aerialist. The show business life of the circus suited him perfectly and influenced his life thereafter. Taught drums and trumpet by his Dad, at age ten Harry was leading the Number Two band in the family's new affiliation, the Christy Circus.

Harry's first major gig was with Ben Pollack, whose band nurtured Glenn Miller, Benny Goodman and Jack Teagarden, among others. Then, from 1937 to 1939, he was a key member of a spectacular trumpet section, alongside Ziggy Elman and Chris Griffin in the Benny Goodman band. By the time of the famed Carnegie Hall concert of January, 1938, Harry was the trumpet idol of a nation of Swing-crazy kids and a year later he was out on his own. I did some dance band radio remotes with James in 1941 and again after the war and began to interview him seriously in 1976. At my suggestion, Lincoln Mayorga, a partner in Sheffield Lab records, chose Harry to record direct-to-disc in the Chapel of the Hollywood First Presbyterian Church and I was there to prepare the liner notes. He was, as usual, in high form. Even after a between-sessions dinner, laced with what seemed to be an endless parade of Beefeater martinis, Harry was in total command and played like a 35-year-old. With no tape recorder to permit re-mixing and editing, each side had to be flawless. Listen to the three-CD collection released by Sheffield in 1990 and you'll hear the results.

Although I came to know his band and his music well, I never thought I truly knew the man. For a fill-in on Harry himself, I turned to his closest associates through all his years of leading his own band, the Monte family. I talked with his Manager, Pee Wee Monte, who had been Benny Goodman's Band Boy, with Pee Wee's wife Vi, who had served as Secretary to the band, and with Pee Wee's brother Sal, Harry's Road Manager. Other Monte brothers, Al and Fred, had also worked for Harry in the early years. To bring us up-to-date, I interviewed Art Depew, leading the band and carrying on the James tradition into the '90s. You'll also find that Helen Forrest, in another chapter, talks at length and with great fondness about her ex-boss.

Harry James was never a musical snob. Here's what he told me:

Harry James

HARRY: To me, there's only two kinds of music, good and bad. If I like it it's good, and if I don't like it, it's bad. If I like it, I play it, and if I don't like it, I don't. And I think that's an opinion shared by most people. You know, you'll have somebody say, "Oh, this rock is terrible." Well, that's not a statement to make because there are a lot of good things, a lot of good tunes and a lot of good tunes in country western. There are a lot of good tunes all over. Back when I first started the band they talked about all the good songs but I never did play *The Three Little*

Bitty Fitty in a Itty Bitty Pool, or any of that stuff either, you know. Because there was bad music then just as much as there is today. It was always real commercial things that I didn't like playing.

FRED: Audience reaction proves that you are right and that's been true no matter what kind of a band you had, like the real swinging jazz oriented first band, and the band that became known as the Sweet Band after the success of *You Made Me Love You* and *I Cried For You* and some other hits like that. Then you had a band that was very avant garde with lots of "bopish" overtones, then back to the swing band. Harry, how do you compare the band of today with the band of ten years ago or twenty years ago? Is it always evolving? Is the musical caliber always the highest?

HARRY: Well, I never compare bands; I always compare nights and if the band is playing good tonight then I am very happy. If it isn't playing good I'm very unhappy, but certainly right now the band's been playing real well. We just finished 38 consecutive days of one-nighters and we had some real tough trips. In fact, we did a concert in Mobile from 3:30 in the afternoon until 5:30 in the afternoon, got on the bus, drove down to New Orleans and did the King Bacchus Festival and worked from 10:00 p.m. to 2:00 a.m. It was enjoyable, the band played good so we didn't mind it.

FRED: Just about every time I've caught the band—any of your bands, right after the theme, the opener has been *Don't Be That Way*.

HARRY: Yeah, I do it everyplace I go because when I was with the great Benny Goodman Band and we did the first Carnegie Hall Concert, the first jazz concert ever held in Carnegie Hall, the first tune we ever played there was *Don't Be That Way*. I've sort of had a little feeling of good luck about it and we play it for the first tune every place that we go.

FRED: What a watershed event that was, January 16, 1938, a cold and wintery night in Manhattan. It made history and, I think, indirectly led to your leaving Benny and going out with your own band and also led to the departure of Gene Krupa to lead his own band. Speaking of drummers, did you start on drums in the circus?

HARRY: I played drums in my father's band before I started playing the trumpet.

FRED: The drum has been very important in your band.

HARRY: It's just like a good quarterback.

FRED: Who's drumming with you now?

HARRY: Les DeMerle, he's been with us for about six seasons now, since Sonny Paine left. We've been very fortunate having Buddy Rich with us for almost eleven years. We've always had such a ball working together because we could sort of feel each other, you know. We did a record *In The Mood* and, for no reason at all, I said, "Hey, Buddy, it comes from my soul, let's go into a Latin thing." We went into a Latin thing. If you ever hear this thing, you wouldn't believe it. We didn't know where we were or anything, we were just playing and playing. All of a sudden we went "zonk" and we were out together and right back into the thing. We could never duplicate it, we could never play it again because there's no way you could count the bars or anything else.

FRED: Was it ever released?

HARRY: Oh, yes, sure, it was an album.

FRED: What label?

HARRY: I think it was Dot because we bought the only copies—so it had to be Dot.

FRED: Of course, Buddy Rich was just one on an almost endless list of great musicians who worked with the Harry James Bands throughout the years and, of course, the same thing was true about the great singers.

HARRY: We were very fortunate in that, when I first heard Sinatra, he was singing out at the Rustic Cabin in Jersey and he joined the band. This was right after I'd organized it and he

HARRY JAMES BAND, the summer of 1939. Harry is center with Connie Haines to the left and Frank Sinatra to the right. Next to Sinatra is Dave Matthews, saxist and major arranger for the James band through the years.

stayed with us for about seven months, I guess. Nancy was pregnant and we weren't making enough money to even pay him the $75 he was supposed to get, so he went with Tommy Dorsey and I said, "Well, if we don't do any better in the next six months or so, try to get me on, too." We were really having a time. But I was very fortunate in all my career by having great singers like Sinatra, then Dick Haymes took his place. Helen Forrest was there and Connie Haines, Kitty Kallen, and Marion Morgan. We were very lucky in having great singers with us all of the time.

FRED: But you had some bad luck once in a while, with record producers. I remember we were talking, not so very long ago, about Columbia Records and you were a little sore at Mitch Miller because, at that time, Columbia had. . .

HARRY: Not just a little—a whole damn bunch.

FRED: . . .had not released many good things of yours. We were talking in particular about *Midnight Sun.*

HARRY: No, it had nothing to do with not releasing things—he wanted me to do some real corny things and I refused to do it, so I left the company. It was that simple.

FRED: You did a few though, like *Castle Rock*, for example.

HARRY: No, that was Sinatra who did that—I just accompanied him.

FRED: Were you pleased with that record?

HARRY: No, I think it was the worst thing either one of us ever did. You ask Sinatra and he'll tell you the same thing.

FRED: Are there still masters in the Columbia files that have never been released?

HARRY: We don't have any idea because most of the things that we did for Columbia were released immediately when we did them. But that's back in the days when they were recording good music and when Mitch came in with the gimmicks and all of this stuff . . . We only did one thing, *Brave Bulls*, that Mitch wanted me to do. I didn't really do a good job of it. It could have been a lot better, but other than that everything else became what he was still trying to do—*Ghost Riders In The Sky*, you know. I just didn't feel like playing that way.

FRED: You were sure one of Columbia Records' biggest artists for a long time, especially during the war years. And you replaced Glenn Miller in that period of time on the Chesterfield radio show, didn't you? That three-night-a-week broadcast coast to coast. You replaced Glenn when he went into the service?

HARRY: Well, the way that happened—we were working out at the Meadowbrook and Miller was doing his last broadcast. He called me about three or four days before and said, "I've recommended you to take over the show." He did such a fantastic job with Chesterfield and, naturally, they would take the first person that he would recommend. So I went on the show with him as their, sort of, a guest, just to say "Hello, Glenn" and "We are going to take your show over next week." He said, "Why don't you do *Jukebox Saturday Night*?" I said, "That's a good idea." So I played that in the thing where they do the "Listen to the music of Harry James" and so forth. So I played that with them and it was the following week that we took over the show and we had the show for, I think, around three years or something like that.

FRED: And here it is about 35 years later and you're still packing them in wherever you go.

HARRY: Well, we've been very fortunate. It seems like people want to hear us, so just about every place that we play we have a nice crowd. It's sort of difficult to say which way a trend is going. I think the only thing wrong with the band business is that we don't have any of the younger kids come up with new bands and they should because with the schools that they have now, with the music programs they have in all the universities with their stage bands and all, you'd think that someone would have the fortitude and the strength to go out and try to fight it, like "Blood, Sweat and Tears" was such a big boost, you know, at the time, because the kids from "Blood, Sweat and Tears" were all

Julliard graduates, which is great, I mean they are great players. But you set guys down and you get four guys in a section; four trumpet players and three trombones and five saxes and four rhythms, and they have to listen to each other just like a ball club. If you don't have a good double play combination on the ball club, you have no ball club.

FRED: What do you see in terms of young musicians in the future, working with big bands? Are you saying there is an opportunity, if they are willing to seek it out?

HARRY: Oh, I think they have the greatest opportunity ever, just like with young athletes. Kids who are only eighteen, nineteen years old now are already playing major league ball, and the same thing is possible for the kids that come out of these stage bands in the different schools and universities, but you can't just sit back and wait for it. You've got to go out and work. You have to make it happen. You don't join a ball club and sit on the bench and say, "Someday I'll be great." You go out and hustle and try to get your job.

FRED: You are a baseball fan pre-eminent, are you not?

HARRY: Definitely, yes.

FRED: It's been said that you used to hire guys primarily because they could play ball.

HARRY: Well, that was secondary. First they had to play music.

FRED: You and Tommy Dorsey and a few of the other bands used to play ball on the road.

HARRY: It's a good outlet for traveling around as much as we did.

FRED: I've heard you called the world's greatest St. Louis Cardinals fan and when you like people you call them a "Card," and when you don't like them you call them a "Dodger" or something else. But is it true that these days you schedule the band around the baseball training camps in the Spring and then baseball games in the summertime and in the fall, be back on the Coast in time for the horse racing?

186

HARRY: We take February and March down South. We start in Texas and we work our way down into Florida and then we end up the last week in Lauderdale at the Galt Ocean Mile Hotel.

FRED: And then you go out, where—you go out in April again?

HARRY: We go back April 18th.

FRED: Where do you head for then?

HARRY: We fly right to Philadelphia and go from there.

FRED: All up and down the Eastern Seaboard?

HARRY: Uh huh, all around the East and we end up around Louisville, Cincinnati, somewhere like that on the way back.

FRED: Members of the band get to play any ball anymore? Do you?

HARRY: Not quite, we've gone past that stage a few years back.

FRED: You still got a mixture of old-timers and youngsters in the band, don't you?

HARRY: Right, I don't care how old a guy is, so long as he can play.

FRED: How do you go about recruiting members of the band?

HARRY: Well, we have a bench of about fifty people waiting to come into the band.

FRED: Uh huh, and these are what people? Graduates of conservatories or people. . .

HARRY: No, sir, these are people that have been working around for a long time and working around town.

FRED: Do you ever find yourself taking anybody right out of school?

HARRY: Nope, I don't have the time or the patience.

FRED: In other words, they've got to sit in and cut the book right away, huh?

HARRY: Well, they don't sit in with this band. We only have one rehearsal a year. If someone is recommended, then I take the recommendation, because we don't make many changes, but when we do—like for instance, our new first trumpet player, Clyde (Reasinger). He recommended the kid that's next to him who is a young graduate from North Texas and he came in and he plays his part. If he didn't, he would be let go after the first date.

AUTHOR'S NOTE: During the Sheffield Lab sessions, I talked to Harry about his recording career, managing to touch on just a few personal favorites.

FRED: Harry, let's talk about records, not necessarily the big hit things, but things you found particularly interesting.

HARRY: Well, I think perhaps the most difficult thing I ever did was *Trumpet Rhapsody* which I wrote. In those days you couldn't redo it, I mean you couldn't splice it. We were doing it on the master and with a two-sided record. If you made one mistake towards the end of it or anywhere during it, you had to do the entire thing over.

FRED: Who did the solo violin on it? I played it just today.

HARRY: A fellow named Glenn Herzer. Now we had two copies of that out. Glenn Herzer did one and Hoyt Bohannon did the other on the trombone, and they had both copies that they released.

FRED: You don't know where I could get hold of a copy of B*oo Woo* and *Woo Woo*, do you?

HARRY: I tell you I don't. That's the first thing I ever made. I was still with Goodman when I recorded that and John Hammond had me do that.

FRED: You made a number of records, didn't you, with Lionel Hampton—some of those late night things?

HARRY: I wrote quite a few things for him. We did eight sides with Lionel at the time that I was with Goodman. I remember one that I wrote for him was *Shoe Shiner's Drag.* I'm amazed at myself, remembering these because my memory only goes to music. We did *Shoe Shiner's Drag* and some other Dixieland tune, I can't remember the name of it. Ziggy Elman made the other tune charts. We did four of them for him.

FRED: *Two O'Clock Jump*—an early hit for you still in the books; I hear you play it, but you play kind of a shortened version.

HARRY: Well, we do the version of it we do all the time on the dance album. We don't extend it too long. You don't want to make them faint while they are dancing.

FRED: The original recording on Columbia really, two sides that actually was this side.

HARRY: No, it wasn't two sides, we never did two sides.

FRED: You did *One O'Clock* and then *Two O'Clock.*

HARRY: That's different. We did *One O'Clock* one year and then about three years later we did *Two O'Clock.* The *One O'Clock Jump* was made with the Count Basie Band. I used some of their guys. The *Two O'Clock Jump* was made with my band about three years later.

FRED: Weren't they released back to back when. . .

HARRY: They could have been on the reissue, but not originally.

FRED: Some of the best records available by you today, and some on CD now, are on the Hindsight label and they are air checks. Also, you recorded two Columbia albums, especially done from dance band remotes, but not air checks, but done specifically for the occasions.

HARRY: We did a thing called One Night Stand at the Aragon Ballroom in Chicago which was the first time that any band had—we did a live broadcast. In fact, we recorded three days, three nights of tapes and then we edited those all in together, and that was the first time that was ever done. Then we did one

HARRY JAMES at Sheffield Lab recording session
in Hollywood, 1974. (Courtesy Sheffield Lab)

from the Palladium which was alive from the stage. My two favorite tracks in that are *Flash* and *Sugar Foot Stomp* with Buddy Rich. We had a ball doing *Flash*, Buddy and I.

FRED: I know you have been particularly proud of the direct-to-disk Sheffield Lab records. It was my lucky break to have suggested you for the date and then to have written the liner notes for the Sheffield Albums. Let me pick a few personal favorites—a very funky piece, *Blues Stay Away*, that has some old time writing for the sax.

HARRY: That was the thing we did originally with Harry James and His Western Friends. In fact, our guitar player was Glen Campbell and it was about five or six months before he made those big hits of his. We also did *San Antonio Rose*.

190

FRED: Where was this? In Vegas?

HARRY: No, we did it in L.A. and we used a string section. In fact, Louie Bellson was the drummer on that. It was fun doing them because I'm from Texas and I've always liked western tunes, the good ones. Glen and I did a thing on *San Antonio Rose* that I really like. We did fours all the way through it and it turned out real good. He's a terrific jazz guitarist, you know.

FRED: I understand that—in every way a great guitarist. A track I never tire of playing, especially because of the bass playing of young Dave Stone, is *More Spludie, Please.*

HARRY: Bob Stone, his father played with us for about twelve years and he didn't want to travel anymore so he went with the Los Angeles Symphony. Almost a year ago we called Bob and said, "Bob we need a bass player, we are going on a trip." I wanted an upright bass and there are so few guys that play anymore. He said, "Have you heard my son?" I said, "No, I haven't, would you recommend him?" He says, "I won't recommend him, you hear him." Well, I find out that he's with Woody Herman for eight years and he was with Kenton (Stan) for almost a year. So I thought that since he was with those two guys, he's got to be able to play. He didn't want to travel that much so he came into town and he's a fantastic player. The cutest thing is that we are doing an Alaskan trip, June 5th for two weeks.

FRED: One of those cruises?

HARRY: Uh huh, on Sitmar, on the Fairsea. We are going up there for two weeks and now they ask us to do an additional two weeks, so little David says, "Oh, good, I'll let my father do the second two weeks because he enjoys those trips so much." So I said, "If you do, make him pay you $50 to do the gig."

FRED: *Opus No. One*, Sy Oliver's tune that was such a hit for Tommy Dorsey and Gene Krupa, as well. How about that arrangement?

HARRY: That's a Bob Florence arrangement and there really isn't too much in it because Bob writes so beautifully for us because, as Ernie Wilkins does, he puts the rests in the right places. Sometimes it's so important to have a rest and then play because it makes the time so much more there, and important. We do quite a few things that Bob Florence did for us. I think he's a very, very intelligent arranger.

FRED: *Sweet Georgia Brown*, you did years ago for Columbia Records, it seems to me, primarily with a small band.

HARRY: You know what, truthfully, I don't even remember doing *Sweet Georgia Brown*. I think that was one of the first arrangements that we had. It must have been number 12 or 13 or 14, with Andy Gibson. He did it for us many years later. I was watching the Globe Trotters one night and they use it for their theme in the beginning and I said, "Gee, people sort of like the Charleston now-a-days 'cause everyone seemed to go back to the old dancing and all." I sketched the whole thing out and Rob (Turk) did it for us. It's strictly a Charleston type of thing, but it swings and we enjoy playing it.

FRED: *Blues For Sale*, I think you recorded it once before, for Capital?

HARRY: Yes, we did *Blues For Sale*. That's also Ernie Wilkins. That, to me is one of the great originals because it doesn't make any difference what age group we play for, they can all dance to *Blues For Sale*. It's in that real good group.

FRED: As a matter of fact, you play a lot of Blues.

HARRY: Oh, yes, I love it. I was brought up in Texas with the Blues. In fact, I was down in what they call barbecue row in Texas, when I was about eleven or twelve years old, playing with the guys that had the broken bottle neck on the guitar and playing the Blues—and that's all we knew. I was brought up with the Blues.

FRED: Among the ballads in the Sheffield Albums, *Lara's Theme* from *Dr. Zhivago* is a stand-out.

HARRY: A very dear friend of mine that I worked with when I was in Texas and I joined Ben Pollack's Band. I got him on the

Band. I joined Benny Goodman's Band and I got him on Benny Goodman's Band. Then he joined me and he's one of the greatest arrangers that ever lived. His name is Dave Matthews, one of the great tenor saxophone players of all time. When we went to Reno, I guess it was eleven or twelve years ago, I said, "Hey, Dave there's a cowboy tune that I want to have an arrangement of." He said, "What is it?" I said, "I don't know, it's something like da-da-da-da." Dave says, "I don't know what that is." Then he says, "You must be an idiot. What cowboy tune? That's the theme from *Dr. Zhivago*." I said, "O.K., write it." So he did this thing on it and he did a real good little two-beat chart on it.

FRED: *Clear Day (On A Clear Day You Can See Forever)*, of course, a great standard and an opportunity for the band to show its section work, it sounded to me.

HARRY: Our trumpet player, Rob Turk, writes quite a bit for us and I asked him to do a Lunceford (Jimmy) type arrangement on *Clear Day*. He's very flexible. He can write any way in the world that you want him to write. I think it turned out pretty good. Its sort of reminiscent of a Lunceford arrangement.

FRED: One heck of a trumpet player, too. I heard you two kidding around with a little Mexican theme there before—was that one finger you were using?

HARRY: Oh, yeah, we both use one finger and play the *Carnival Of Venice*, and one of these days we'll record it in duet.

AUTHOR'S NOTE: To better understand James personally, let's turn now to an interview done in the late Spring of 1990 with long-time James band manager, Pee Wee Monte, his wife, Vi, and his brother, Sal. On Harry's death they became Chairman, Secretary and President of the still-continuing Harry James Band, under an agreement with Harry's five children of three marriages.

Sal Monte, Pee Wee Monte and Vi Monte

Pee Wee had started as a sax player with Larry Funk (Vaughn Monroe was his roommate) and Frank Dailey, then joined Hal Kemp, from whose band he says he was "kidnapped" to become Benny Goodman's Band Boy along about 1936, joining James in 1939 to become Personal Manager. Vi, a bobby-soxer fan of Harry's who, along with thousands of other kids haunted the Paramount Theater in New York when the James crew was in residence, became Secretary to the band in 1943, replacing Pee Wee's brother, Fred. Sal came aboard in 1946. His initial job, he says, was to just "hang out with Harry" at the races and bars and ballparks. Says Sal of those days, "Harry had one rule for the boys in the band, 'no drinking **off** the job!'" Another Monte brother, Al, had been with the band "before there was a band" and had directly brought in the rest of the family. We talked in Vi and Pee Wee's comfortable cabana out by the pool in the San Fernando Valley.

FRED: Let me ask you each and I'll start with you, Sal. Just tell me about Harry, what kind of a guy he was, in general—to be with, to work with, to be around, as a musician, as businessman, as a leader of men.

SAL: As a musician, one of the greatest in the world, what Harry did, his horn, everything. As a business-man, forget it! I'm going to be right out here. Harry's whole philosophy in life, as far as I'm concerned, I don't know whether Vi will agree with it, he loved his freedom even though he was married. He still loved his freedom. Hey, he liked his music, he liked his women, he loved gambling, he had a racing stable, he and Betty Grable. Gambling was a big part of his life. Women were a big part of his life. Music! That afforded him his living so he could have his women and his gambling, and so forth.

FRED: How about baseball?

SAL: Well, baseball, too, but baseball was probably number four, you know. I think there were three ahead of that. Baseball and the St. Louis Cardinals was the number one club. But I loved Harry. Harry always told it like it was. He never hemmed and hawed. If he had to tell a promoter off for good reason, not for any other reason, but he had a valid reason, he would tell that man off. He wouldn't kowtow, take back and say—well, man, he's paying me my salary for tonight so I better be nice to him. If Harry was right, he was right! But I've got to believe, too—many, many times Harry was wrong. He still thought he was right, you understand? But, all in all, he just loved life. O.K., let's leave it right there, he just loved life, but the way **he** wanted to live it.

FRED: Vi, your view of Harry, from a different perspective?

VI: I see Harry very much the way Sal sees him, but I see beyond his talent which is the top and all the musicians felt that way about him. I see him as a very deep, deep person. He harbored very deep thoughts. To go beyond Sal, he was the kind of person you could never lie to. He could never tolerate it if you ever lied to him; he would carry that grudge forever. He would really carry that grudge and always remember that you would lie.

He loved animals. He could not stand cruelty of any kind. If he looked out of a window and saw a dog chained or something that looked like cruelty to him, it would upset him, it ruined his day. He was very considerate of people. He was very sincere in that. He also, which is overlooked a lot, had a tremendous sense of humor. Because he was a very quiet introvert, it wasn't always apparent.

FRED: Pee Wee, you're the quiet member of this family, so let me pose a few specific questions about Harry. When did he leave Benny Goodman?

PEE WEE: January 25, 1939.

FRED: Was it on a friendly basis?

PEE WEE: I guess. He was financed by Goodman to start his band.

FRED: Did Benny then have a piece of the band?

PEE WEE: He had a good piece of the band. I loaned Harry the money to buy Goodman out.

FRED: So you didn't keep a piece of the band then?

PEE WEE: No. We were very close friends.

FRED: By the time he left Benny, Harry had become quite a hero to Swing fans. Who was **his** idol? What trumpet player?

PEE WEE: Louis Armstrong was his boy.

VI: You have to stop and think that, although Harry was raised in Texas, he had a **true** circus background, plus his father, Everett, was born in New Orleans. Now Everett brought a lot of New Orleans type music to Harry. Everett was his first teacher, his only teacher, so he had a marvelous collection of influence that Harry drew from—his circus, his father, his New Orleans background plus the jazz that was prevalent at the time, all of that. He had the most marvelous memory of anybody I know. He incorporated everything. I think he did everything great, I really do.

PEE WEE: There's 2200 arrangements in our book, 2200. He knew every one, note for note, not only his part, but everybody's part.

FRED: How did Harry go about choosing side men for that first band, Sal?

SAL: Well, he initially contacted his Texas friends. Isn't that the way it was, Pee Wee? Didn't he get hold of his Texas buddies to come up to start the band?

PEE WEE: Yes.

SAL: All Texans. Claude Lakey, Claude Bowen, Dalton Rizzotto, Jack Gardner—all the guys—he called them up from Texas.

FRED: Let's jump ahead from those very happy times to the saddest of times—April of 1983. You were on the road with him, Sal, so you probably know as well as anyone. His cancer had been diagnosed and he was a very sick guy.

SAL: He had two gigs in Denver that he wanted to go to and the doctor says, "No way, it's a mile high and how the hell can you breathe?" He finally did make those two trips to those two dates in Denver. I pre-arranged oxygen tanks for his hotel rooms and also at the gig. But he never took one whiff of oxygen, He was very, very strong and he had a will that was unreal. His last gig was at the Century Plaza on June 26th. He was so sick he'd go out there and play and leave it to the piano and come back-stage and put his head down over his arms. He played the gig June 26th and went to the airport. His girl at the time took him to the airport right after the gig, where he took the first plane back to Vegas. As soon as he arrived in Vegas, that doctor put him in the hospital and he never came out.

FRED: I know he died on July 5th and that was a date of some special significance, wasn't it?

SAL: His anniversary, his and Betty Grable's anniversary. Betty Grable passed away ten years earlier and was buried on July 5. All these fives came into play and he died on July 5th.

VI: He said, "If I can just get past July 5th."

SAL: He told that to Viola and to Vickie, his daughter—"If I can only get past July 5"—and, by golly, at around 5:00 that morning he was gone.

AUTHOR'S NOTE: Harry's records continued to sell and his family decided to carry on. When it was decided that the band would resume with some other trumpet-playing leader out front, Art Depew, who had played first trumpet with Harry for four years, was approached. He and the Montes couldn't agree on terms so Joe Graves, who had done Harry's solos, note-for-note, in the Time-Life "Big Band Era" re-creations, was hired for the job. But, by 1988, the Montes and Art had mutually decided to compromise and Art took over. In July of that year

I brought the band to Santa Barbara to appear at a dance promotion for my radio station, KKSB. The band played with polish and Depew, playing great horn, was an affable leader. In 1990 he was still at it, with the band playing casuals, one-nighters, Disneyland and an occasional show with a star of the magnitude of Rosemary Clooney. Sal and Pee Wee refused to make any compromise in the price of the band, in its mode of travel (by deluxe bus) or housing (good hotels). It remained a class act, with a stable membership, doing honor to Harry's memory.

Art Depew

FRED: I take it you have a long-term admiration for Harry James.

ART: Oh, yes, I started as a youth and when he was with Benny Goodman, I fell in love with Harry's playing. I liked all of the players, Charlie Shavers, Ziggy Elman, all wonderful players— of course, Louie Armstrong was the grandfather of all of us. Harry's style intrigued me the most because it was not only good jazz, it was also lyrical. He could turn around and be very lyrical, very soulful, very melodic, as well as playing this wild jazz that he could play. An incredible musician.

FRED: Now you are playing his solos. Are you making a point to play the original solos or are you doing your own improvisations?

ART: In certain places that would be true. For example, I try to go as closely as I can to the original style and flavor of *You Made Me Love You* and on *Two O'Clock Jump* I play his original solo. I do that because that's become the melody of that tune, you see. But when we play things like *Don't Be That Way*, when the trumpet makes its first jazz entrance I just play what I want to play, but in the flavor of Harry James because I like that flavor. I feel that it's called for and it's appropriate and I feel that it's worthwhile doing, so to the best of my ability I try to get in the style of Harry James whenever possible.

198

FRED: I know that you have some old-timers as well as some newcomers with the band. Harry was famous for his loyalty and the loyalty for his side men toward him.

ART: I recall when I was with the brass section, I added up the amount of time that each of us had been on the band, the four trumpet players in the section plus Harry. It came to somewhere around ninety years. That included Nick Buono, who had been with the band at that time almost from the earliest days and then, Harry. Another trumpet player had been with the band ten years, another fourteen years, and I was with the band four years. Add all those up together, including Harry, and we had quite an impressive array of men who had played in the band.

FRED: How do you decide what to play? I realize that you have to play certain things that people expect, but do you dig deep at all into those wonderful Ray Conniff and other things that were done for the band?

ART: You have given part of the answer—all the wonderful things that people expect us to play. We start with that as a framework and what I do, I try to produce the evening. Of course, the opening theme—then we go into *Don't Be That Way* which is the opener, since it was Harry's thing to play that. Then I bounce up the tempo to keep the people interested, keep the mood shifting, the tempo shifting, keep the dancers happy, and keep a feeling of show business, an ongoing feeling of tempo excitement in the evening, that's the way it's done.

FRED: You play a lot of Dixie, don't you? Personally, you enjoy that and you have a little group that works around.

ART: I do a lot of Dixieland jobs. I'm sometimes the leader and sometimes the side man. It's something I learned to do quite a bit of and I learned a lot of the tunes. You have to know those tunes, you know. If somebody says *Fidgety Feet,* you had better know it. You can't fake your way through it. Some of these tunes have a lot of sections to them, but Dixieland is one of the things I like to do.

FRED: There's not a heck of a lot of that in the James band, although there were some echoes of it from time to time.

ART: Oh, yes, Harry was originally a traditional jazz player. We all came from Dixieland Jazz, without any question, although some people don't like the term Dixieland, we were jazz band players, you know. Matty Matlock was the type of artist who would get very upset if they called him a Dixieland musician. "I play in a jazz band" is what he said. But jazz has many forms and many faces and Harry was one of them. Everybody thinks that Jazz that came from the Louis Armstrong era and they reinterpreted it. That's what we are all doing. Yes, you could say that Dixieland influences the jazz that we play.

FRED: I know that Pee Wee Monte is booking the band and his brother, Sal, is the road manager and they take care of a lot of the details, but it would seem to me that it must be a heavy chore heading up a band like that, of the Harry James group.

ART: I am guiding the band, so to speak, but I have a bunch of men in there who know the style implicitly and thoroughly and they love to play that way. I'm trying to make the band not only musically the way it was before, but to give it a feeling of show business, where we are not only playing well but we are getting the people to like us.

FRED: When you get into *Trumpet Blues*—to me that was the highlight of any evening with the James band.

ART: I remember when I first joined the band, I tried out in the Zender Ballroom. Do you remember the Zender Ballroom? It's now a parking lot. It's near the Statler Hotel downtown, or the Hilton Hotel, if you will. They took me up and I played with the band and they gave me this rather nondescript looking part. It looked like the Dead Sea Scroll and it said *Trumpet Blues* on it, and they said, "Would you mind looking this over? Here's where you play, you'll be splitting the lead with Harry." I said O.K. and I took it home for about a week. The next time we played it we were on Long Island in New York City, and Harry said *Trumpet Blues* and all of the trumpet players started down front. Then

HARRY JAMES, Circa 1980. Less hair, more weight, still swinging.

they said, "Oh, wait a minute, we got a new man." I said, "Let's go!" I had memorized it, of course, which was no trick at all, any trumpet player could do it. But Harry never forgot that I had taken the time to memorize *Trumpet Blues*. He never forgot and he was touched by it. So from then on we got along fine.

FRED: Art, you are doing a lot of other things, I know. For example, you are a contractor down here. This must take a lot of your time and a lot of your energy. Are you finding it worthwhile? Are you finding it exciting and challenging?

ART: Very challenging. In the first place, I've tried to play like Harry all of my life. There are times when I've had to play otherwise, you know. I've been a commercial trumpet player, I worked in network TV with Lawrence Welk for eight years and I worked Ray Anthony's band. I've worked with a lot of other bands and I have to play the style that's required at that time. But basically, essentially, I like to play that style and sound and flavor, the lyrical sound. So I find it very exciting. I have a wonderful band as a backdrop, so who could ask for anything more?

AUTHOR'S NOTE: In my final interview with Harry, I asked him what plans he might have to retire.

HARRY: To retire to what? If I were retired I'd do exactly what I'm doing. I have my horses and I go see baseball games and I play music that I like.

FRED: And that's all you need.

HARRY: There's no time for anything else.

Harry James left a legacy of hundreds of records, on Columbia, Savoy (reissues of Varsity sides), Capitol, Dot, MGM, Verve, Sheffield Lab and a few other labels. As this was being written, numerous reissues in CD form were being added to the record store shelves. I've listed some few albums and CDs I treasure in the back of this book. I hope you'll be able to locate many of them.

11

TONY BENNETT

Tony Bennett first recorded *Boulevard of Broken Dreams* in 1950. In 1990 Columbia released his newest album, *Astoria: Portrait of the Artist*, which included a brand new version of *Boulevard*. If you compare the two versions, you'll notice a certain mellow edge in the later version, a quality that maturity does not always bring to a singer. The voice itself is as sure, as strong and as certain of its style as it ever was, perhaps even more of a perfectly-controlled instrument. The selection of material reflects the unerring good taste typical of this performer. Great standards like *Body and Soul, Speak Low,* and *The Folks That Live on the Hill.* There are classy new songs, including one written about Tony's daughter, Antonia. Everything is approached with the intense involvement of an artist who lives for his work.

Bennett went through some slow times, even a period when many felt his singing had been impaired by personal problems and the pressures of a music industry by then indifferent to quality performers. None of that shows in his fourth decade as a major artist. "Artist" has a second meaning for Tony, of course, for he is an accomplished painter, whose canvases are displayed in some of our best museums. It's a subsidiary talent but not a minor one.

The principal interview with Tony that follows took place in September of 1982 in Los Angeles. In September of 1990, his career had clearly developed a second-wind as he toured the world, playing to capacity audiences and continued to produce, although not as frequently as many of us would like, albums done on his own terms, with his own choice of superb musicians. Astoria-born Anthony Dominick Benedetto had come a long way and remained solidly on course.

FRED: Columbia Records has always been your principal home. As I understand it, it was home in more ways than one to you. That is to say its location in the middle of downtown Manhattan?

TONY: Yes, my father was an Italian immigrant and he was smart enough to open up a grocery store right on those grounds, right on 52nd Street and Sixth Avenue.

FRED: Your early scuffling days as a singer were in New York?

TONY: Oh yes, all the way. Seven tough years, very tough years.

FRED: Starting when?

TONY: Well, right after the war. I was in the Second World War in France and Germany. When I came out I joined the GI Bill of Rights and joined the American Theater Wing and had some very good teachers there. But nevertheless, it was difficult getting a job, finding work.

FRED: Using another name in the beginning, I understand.

TONY: Yeah, right, in those days they wanted to get a name that was quick enough that anyone could remember, you know. So I had a name, Joe Bari and it was quickly changed by Bob Hope. Bob saw me and he said, "What's your real name?" I said, "Anthony Dominick Benedetto." He said, "Let's Americanize it and call you Tony Bennett."

TONY BENNETT in concert with the Count Basie band.
(Ray Avery photo)

FRED: Just like that.

TONY: Yup.

FRED: And so you stuck with it.

TONY: Well, I like it. You know, it's a lucky name for me because Bob took me on the road with Les Brown's band and it was something that was unforgettable in my life. It was my introduction to the big-time and I couldn't think of a nicer introduction.

FRED: I didn't know you'd had that experience with a big band. Seems to me that would be something a singer would miss, not having grown up working with big bands.

TONY: Well, I know I missed it because I adored all the bands, Charlie Barnet, Jimmy Lunceford, all the great bands. And so it became quite eccentric but after the war the bands broke up, but when I finally got a little reputation and someone said, "Who would you like to play with?" I'd quickly say Count Basie or Woody Herman or Duke Ellington.

FRED: Two fine albums came out of that desire to work with the big bands that I know about, both with Basie. One was done live, wasn't it? In a club in Philadelphia?

TONY: Yes, in the Latin Casino.

FRED: Fine, fine album. Wasn't that with Roulette (Records)? Then Columbia made one?

TONY: Columbia was the live one and Roulette did it right, as far as I'm concerned. That was really traditional Basie and the band was set up right and it was very well recorded. I'm very happy with both albums, but the one I really prefer is the one on Roulette.

FRED: You've been very fortunate in your choice of conductors through the years, for example, Robert Farnon.

TONY: Well, Farnon, he's who Quincy Jones and Johnny Mandell and Don Costa call "the governor." He's the best orchestrator around.

FRED: And apparently the most sympathetic to the performer, the singer.

TONY: Oh, yes, he did albums with Lena Horne and Sinatra and the Singers Unlimited. George Shearing just recently did a beautiful album with him.

FRED: George sent me a copy of that.

TONY: Isn't that magnificent?

FRED: Just absolutely, shatteringly beautiful.

TONY: You know that version of *Last Night When We Were Young,* which David Rose considers the best song ever written, George Shearing was clever enough to put a little beat behind it. It's always been a dilemma to me, as much as I love the song and feel it—it feels kind of slow when you sing it. You feel like maybe you are not really getting the audience and might be putting them to sleep. It was so clever of George Shearing to put this simple walk and this nice little beat behind it. It made the song come alive. Someday I'd like to sing it that way.

FRED: Didn't you do a concert around 1972 in London with Farnon?

TONY: Yes, that was my greatest musical experience because it was the 100th Anniversary of Royal Albert Hall, which is a big thing in Britain for everyone there. It was with the London Philharmonic, the first time I ever sang with a Philharmonic orchestra, and it was Robert Farnon conducting. It was really unforgettable. BBC recorded it and Vaughan Littlewood is the directoress. They made a beautiful television show of it.

FRED: Great album. I think Johnny Bunch is the piano player on it. And ten years before that you were at Carnegie Hall?

TONY: Yes, that was the very first concert I ever did and it was something! It's not on the liner notes but Arthur Penn, the great theater and film director, directed that concert at Carnegie Hall.

FRED: Choreographed it, so to speak.

TONY: Yes, he set the lights up and made sure that everybody was relaxed, as much as possible, because it was my very first concert.

FRED: And were you relaxed?

TONY: More or less. My knees were going quite a bit, but then it felt good after a while.

FRED: You've made albums with all sizes of groups. The ones I admire the most are those done with a limited number of musicians, particularly the Bill Evans album. That was on your own label wasn't it?

TONY: Yes, that was on Improv (Records) and also one on Fantasy (Records), the two albums we made. That was a great experience because Bill told me to keep all the cronies home and just go up with him to San Francisco and it was just he and I. For three or four days we just went over it and had a beautiful little musicale.

FRED: I don't think there was anybody quite like Evans and probably never will be.

TONY: I feel the same way. Stepping away from anything intellectual, when it comes to classical music, I could listen to Ravel all day long and be very happy, and not get bored with it. And I feel the same way about Bill Evans music. I could put his music on all day long and never tire of it.

FRED: The impressionistic. . .

TONY: Yes, impressionistic music, I migrate to that.

FRED: Then quite different, you worked with Ruby Braff and George Barnes?

TONY: Ruby is just dynamite. I can't believe the state of mind that he's in right now. He's knocking off one great album after another. He just did a great album that's a salute to Sinatra, which is a beautiful album. Now he's doing an album of classical pieces with Dick Hyman.

FRED: He did a great salute to Fred Astaire, also.

TONY: Oh, yes, he does beautiful work. He's such a great musician.

FRED: It's clear that you've associated yourself with great musicians and they have associated themselves with you.

TONY: Like Harold Land and Billy Exiner and Zoot Sims and Al Cohen, just one great musician after another.

FRED: Were you able to ask for and get the kind of people you wanted, pretty much from the beginning, or did it take some years of getting established before you were able to call for this kind of talent?

TONY: A lot of them came to me and said they'd like to do something. Stan Getz said, "Gee, I'd love to make some records with you and we did."

FRED: What records did you make with Stan?

TONY: We did *Danny Boy* and *You're Clear Out of This World*. Old standards, but beautiful, just beautiful. Herbie Hancock and Alvin Jones were on that date. These are the great surprises because Stan would say to me, "Why don't we make some records together?" It wasn't really planned, I just walked in to listen to Stan Getz's record date and I was in the booth and he said, "Come on, Tony, come out here and sing some tunes with us." That's how it went down. You know it's funny, I've always been around beautiful musicians. The first album I ever made was with Chuck Wayne and the second album was a thing called "Tony." On that album it says Ray Conniff and his orchestra, because I was pretty new and didn't know what I know now. But, actually he ended up conducting the orchestras. We had people that were unknown at that time, to the general public, but we had a selection of arrangers that you wouldn't believe. We had Marion Evans, Gil Evans, Neal Hefti, Ralph Burns, Marty Manning and Percy Faith. They're all on one album and it just said Ray Conniff and his orchestra. To this day I really feel bad that they didn't get proper credit on that album.

FRED: Do you have any choices of tunes from that first album?

TONY: Yes, I liked *These Foolish Things*.

FRED: Great album. The early hits you had though, were mostly not classic type ballads, but some of them seem to stand up, *Firefly* or *Rags To Riches*. Do you get tired of those things?

TONY: Yeah. A little earlier we did some beautiful things like *I Won't Cry Anymore* and *Blue Velvet*. The first time I ever felt I had my eye and ear on the whole idea of recordings is when Ella Fitzgerald—I took my Mom to see Ella Fitzgerald at Birdland, she was my Mother's favorite singer, and mine too—said, "I love the way you sing that *Blue Velvet*." That was the first time and I said, "Wow, Ella Fitzgerald saying that!" That was really something!

FRED: Who, among other singers, did you admire when you began to sing professionally yourself?

TONY: The one who hypnotized all the musicians in New York in those days was Billie Holiday. But I loved a lot of the pop singers, of course. Nat King Cole was so different. He came in and whispered, he was the first guy who really sang intimately and to me that was the proper way to be an intimate singer. Of course, the big influence was Bing Crosby and then I fell in love with Frank Sinatra. We would go and play hooky and catch him at the Paramount Theater and catch four or five shows a day at the Paramount. Those were the great days with Buddy Rich playing, and with Jo Stafford, who's a magnificent singer and contributed so much on recordings, to the art of popular singing.

FRED: The record business, I don't have to tell you, is so mercurial. Today it makes you want to cry when you think of everything that's in the archives that's not available. Yet you've been luckier than some, I think, in that respect.

TONY: Somehow or other I think the companies should find a way of coming out with a nice popular price brand of all those catalogued performances. I think it would really, really start a big fire from a little spark, if they did that. The public is just waiting for that product on classic performers and they don't get it. They walk in and they see all these new albums that are being pushed and the record stores get a lot of returns. They get quite disappointed. But they would never get disappointed if they heard Louis Armstrong or Benny Goodman, those master-pieces at Carnegie Hall that he did with the great Gene Krupa and Teddy Wilson. I think the record companies would be in for a big surprise if they unleashed their catalog and made those the popular records of the day.

FRED: What happened with your own label? Unable to find distributorship?

TONY: Exactly. Yes, that's what happened. But I was very happy with the artistic worth of Earl "Fatha" Hines and Charlie Bird, Bill Evans, Ruby Braff, people like that. Marion McPartland, my partner. They were all on that label and it was really a joy to have all those great sounds coming out of my own label.

FRED: Do you play an instrument, Tony?

TONY: No, I don't.

FRED: Never. Did you ever study?

TONY: I study music all of the time and I'd like to study piano. I failed completely on guitar. I tried for two or three years, but on the road it's really difficult not having a proper teacher to show you the rudiments. It was quite difficult. But I'll get to the piano.

FRED: How do you go about choosing the material for recording and for performances? There are so many sad songs around these days. Unrequited love is the underlying theme of most of them and yet you find some very positive things to sing about.

TONY: Yeah, I'm kind of gravitating away from real tough torch songs. They are beautifully performed and well written, but they kind of leave a real down touch of sadness in the performance. I'm trying to get away from that recently.

FRED: You never stop singing *Love Is Here To Stay*?

TONY: No. That is my favorite song.

FRED: You did some records and I think appeared with, considerably, Candido. That was at a time when bongos and beyond was getting to be a national rage.

TONY: Well, you know I had this, what I felt, and a lot of musicians felt, was a tremendous stigma. In my early career they wanted me to record with these lush sweet sounds and leave it at that. If I brought up a rhythm idea, a jazz influenced idea, as a popular singer, they resented it and they said, "No, don't change. This would be too much of a shock to the public." Al Ham was daring enough to say, "Come on, let's. . ." Well, originally it was Ralph Sharon who said, "Hey, come on let's get with it. You sing jazz, so why not do it?" And he put up this idea, made a concept album. Ralph did the arrangements of all the flutes and the trombones for the rhythm section. But that rhythm section was changed with every band, with all different drummers. We had Jo Jones, Candido, Sabu, Billy Exiner and Art Blakey, just so many of them on this one album. It was called "The Beat of My Heart" album. That really opened up a whole lot.

FRED: *Crazy Rhythm*, was that on that album?

TONY: *Crazy Rhythm*. Right. That's the one that Jazzbeaux Collins plays in New York. It opened up a whole new audience for me and a whole new vitality in my career.

FRED: Individual songs have done that for you, too. Johnny Mercer's *I Wanna Be Around* comes to mind. How did that reach you?

TONY: He got it to me. Sadie Vammerstedt, a housewife from Youngstown, Ohio, was a big fan of Johnny Mercer and she wrote him this letter saying, "I wanna be around to pick up the pieces when somebody breaks your heart. Now that little bit of philosophy sounds just like you, Johnny. I'd love to have you round it out. I'm an amateur song writer who loves song writing. I'd love to have a professional like you finish the song." So he gave her fifty percent of the song. He got it to me and, of course, we were riding on *I Left My Heart In San Francisco* and then the next side that we came out with was *I Wanna Be Around.* So she took one heck of a ride. And all because that song was a backup to another hit and we had two hits in a row. Every once in a while I'd be singing in some cabaret or some concert hall and I'd see someone waving in the audience, I'd look twice and it'd be Sadie Vammerstedt.

FRED: Ginger Mercer was telling me that Sadie used to write or telephone Johnny every little bit and say, "I'm going to be on this show and that show. They want to interview me here and there." She called up one time and she says, "This is getting to be just **too** much!" (Laughter) That was a song for which Johnny wrote both words and music. He was something very special, of course, among song writers and I gather that you were as fond of his work as I.

TONY: I'm not a literary critic at all. I love to read, but I'll tell you one thing, I think he was America's greatest poet. And I know that a lot of people in the literary world would say, "Wait a minute. How dare you say that?" But I just fall in love, I mean anybody could make up phrases like 'My huckleberry friend' in *Moon River* or make a brand new word that's never been used before like 'Dreamily.' He was just an astounding talent, beside being a great human being. I just hope someday that someone does justice in making a film or play on Broadway about his life because he was **really** Americana, true Americana.

FRED: Yes, he was. You sang a lot of his songs. I think of *One For The Road* immediately. Still do that?

TONY: Yes, still do that. And Sinatra still does it and it was written originally for Fred Astaire.

FRED: Sure, I remember the scene in the bar.

TONY: I do too. It's really something.

FRED: I saw it in the rain in the South Pacific sitting on a hill. I think they screened it over there for the Armed Services before it showed here.

TONY: Wow! I love Arlen (Harold) and so I end up doing all those Arlen songs.

FRED: Sure. *Blues In The Night*.

TONY: *Come Rain or Come Shine, Somewhere Over The Rainbow,* and *Black Magic* which Johnny Mercer wrote. You know a song that Johnny Mercer wrote called *Harlem Butterfly*?

FRED: Sure! I've got a Maxine Sullivan record of it.

TONY: Isn't that wonderful?

FRED: I've got to ask you about *San Francisco*. How did that song come to your attention?

TONY: Ralph Sharon, once again. He's found all my songs for me, right through the seasons. And he knew these fellows, George Cory and Douglass Cross from San Francisco. They wrote a lot of songs for Billie Holiday. We were in Hot Springs, Arkansas, on our way up to San Francisco and he said, "This would be a nice special song. The people in that town really love their city. Let's do a song about that city." The bartender turned around to us and he said, "You record that song and I'm going to go out and buy a record of that." That was a kind of a tipoff, although I didn't realize how big it would become. I thought it would just be kind of a local hit for the people who love the city so much. But it's funny how it has become such a strong evergreen through the years.

FRED: I guess that's there's just no way you can do a performance without singing that song.

TONY: No. I wouldn't be able to get out of town, any town, without doing that. That's actually the reason people come to see me. I have been sold out ever since that song has come out. So I am really grateful to the song. Everybody asks me the cliche question, "Don't you ever get tired of it?" Finally some press agent in London had me come up with the correct answer to that. I always say to an interviewer, "Do **you** get tired of making love?" and it stops them cold. That's how I feel about that song. It's a good musical song and gets the audience all enthused and makes them feel uplifted, and that's the whole idea of performing anyway.

FRED: Who, among contemporary writers of songs, do you admire and enjoy? We have a mutual friend in Gene Lees; I gather you like Gene's writing.

TONY: Oh yes, and there's Cy Coleman and Stephen Sondheim. Contemporaries like Stevie Wonder and Paul McCartney, I like. There's a big group out there that really are creative writers.

FRED: A lot of creative people around haven't had anything published or performed **new** from them in twenty years, and they're still alive and still writing. We had a session with Jimmy Van Heusen not so long ago. In Palm Springs, he showed me, not just a music bench full, but a whole closet full of songs. Here's a guy who has written, how many?—I don't know, hundreds and hundreds of hits. Same thing's true of Harry Warren.

TONY: How about Irving Berlin?

FRED: And you talk about Harold Arlen. I wonder if it would be possible to search out some of these things, Tony. Maybe sometime do an album with new songs by great artists like that.

TONY: Hey, you know that's a wonderful concept. That really is a clever concept.

FRED: You could sure do it. Hoagy Carmichael was in the same spot. I don't believe that somebody is all of a sudden going to stop writing great tunes like that. It's just the industry that changed.

Tony Bennett

TONY: Just today on the news, I'm really not into politics, but there was this real elder statesman, one of the great Senators who was saluted today on television that I was watching. He's 84 years old and they really heralded him as one of the great statesmen of America, and he said, "The problem is that they've pitted the old against the young in this country. Why should we be in competition with this? Why shouldn't we be properly involved, so that we all work together?" You know, use the wisdom of the old like they do in a lot of countries that have an older culture. They understand. They go to the elder statesmen to find out what to do.

FRED: There's a continuity there.

TONY: Yes. They have all that great experience. They've lived longer. It's just common sense. These people have lived lives. They know the answers. They've been around, they know what's happening. So it's great for the youth to go to the old-timers and say, "What do you think I should do here?" The old-timers have learned how to become economical about things, in the way of being precise and concise about what they are saying, doing, every move counts. Youth can take a big lesson from that.

FRED: My experience is that there is getting to be more and more of a cross-over audience. With my **Swing Thing** show all over the country, I get a lot of letters and a lot of cards from young people, college kids particularly.

TONY: You know, I feel that this is happening. I feel the same change as a performer. The young adults today are starting to like all kinds of music. Where years ago if it wasn't one of their own age, they'd get turned off. It didn't really come from the youngsters. It came from the advertisers and the marketing people. It became a marketing thing. Once the age of computers came in they figured, we don't have to wait and listen to what the audience wants, we'll just kind of force it down their throats. They just felt that whatever was advertised the most would just be sold on impulse. So they had kind of an obsolescence viewpoint instead of the way, originally records were made. They

216

were supposed to be made to last forever. Like Bunny Berigan's *I Can't Get Started With You* as a prime example. Then in 1953, the whole music world changed and they went with selling on impulse. Something that could be replaced quite easily, every two weeks, something new.

FRED: Who staged that?

TONY: It was the major companies. They had all this great, brand new, what they felt was miraculous equipment and they were going to change the premise of handmade things, you see. They said, "Forget quality. We just want sales. We need more, more, more." The first time I heard that, it was quite obscene. I said, "Wait a minute, what's happening?" And then it didn't work, now it's come about, this is a good fifteen, seventeen years later and it just didn't work. I know I was kind of a young pioneer at CBS with Goddard Lieberson and Mitch Miller and Percy Faith in those early days where every record counted. I followed Billie Holiday into the studio and we were always in the black. We never made a stupid financial move.

FRED: It didn't cost that much to make a record, too, in those days.

TONY: We did four sides in 3-1/2 hours. And they were all standards. They are all still played on the radio. Billie Holiday's records are still played on the radio more than ever. And it's amazing how you hear some of these deals. Some companies spend as much as two hundred to three hundred thousand dollars for one album and they really can't finish it. That's the strangest thing I've ever run into. I consider it terrible business.

FRED: Can you, if you get back into the record business, do the things you want to do again, you think?

TONY: Oh yes. That's why I held out so long. I just won't compromise and if I never record again, fine. Luckily enough, the public likes to come and see me. And there's this great medium, television. I go on and get national coverage that way.

FRED: You do a lot of PBS shows?

TONY: Yes. About once a year we do a special.

FRED: And then they show it many times, luckily.

TONY: Yes, right.

FRED: How about clubs? Vegas has kind of gotten to be a big-show type thing without a name star.

TONY: That's because they put it in the hands of the marketing boys and they're in trouble. Up in Tahoe, it's all right because Mr. Harrah had a nice philosophy and has influenced all the other clubs in the area. In Reno, it's all right, Atlantic City is O.K. because it has 30 million people to draw from. But Vegas is in trouble and I think they have to get back to the pros, the people who really know how to put on a show.

FRED: Are you still having fun performing in general, Tony?

TONY: I happen to like it. Hanging out with Ruby, he kind of taught me to eliminate all this kind of smart guy attitude that everybody thinks is fashionable. I kind of imitated him because he said he couldn't wait to just get to work onstage at night. He warms up all day long and hits the stage and really entertains people. He tries to make them feel good. I kind of psych myself out to feel that way and it feels good. It's healthy for me, too, because I try to contribute as much as possible.

FRED: And your sons are working with you.

TONY: My sons have been managing me for the last three years. They have their own group, a rock group called "Neon" and they sing wonderfully. They have great voices and I'm really proud of them because they are nice, respectful people and they have done a magnificent job with handling my career and getting it all straightened out.

MUSIC RESOURCES

In this section you will find a Discography, some suggested books and a list of sources for special and rare items. The Discography lists Compact Discs and Cassettes in most cases, since very few Long Playing records are being produced. Where I've known of vinyl records being available, I've noted them (LP). In the case of some artist with a tremendous number of recordings, I've chosen my favorites and definitive collections. The books include some standard references, biographies and recent publications that I find of special value or that are especially entertaining. It's a compilation that is by no means complete and is confined to presently in-print volumes. Each major city has rare-record stores and I would suggest the Yellow Pages for any serious collector. Of the major chain records stores, the only one I know that stocks, in depth, big bands and the prestigious ballad singers is Tower Records and only in their key San Francisco and Los Angeles (Sunset Blvd.) stores. It must be said, however, that the advent of the Compact Disc (CD) has led even the run-of-the-mill, hot-on-rock music store to carry **some** jazz and big bands. Wear your ear-muffs.

SOURCES

AUDIOPHILE, CIRCLE, JAZZOLOGY RECORDS, 1206 Decatur St., New Orleans, LA 70116. Definitive collection of broadcast transcriptions offered on LP and CD, plus much traditional jazz and vocal artists.

CHIAROSCURO RECORDS, 830 Broadway, New York, NY 10003. Mainstream and traditional jazz, including many recent recordings.

CONCORD JAZZ RECORDS, PO Box 845, Concord, CA 94522. The largest producer of mainstream jazz today, plus vocal artists like Mel Torme and Rosemary Clooney.

CORINTHIAN RECORDS, PO Box 6296, Beverly Hills, CA 90212. Paul Weston and Jo Stafford offer many of their own original recordings, as well as others produced by Weston.

HINDSIGHT RECORDS, PO Box 7114-R, Burbank, CA 91510. Radio air-checks and transcriptions by most of the big bands and great singers.

JAZZ ARCHIVES, 1800 No. Beverly Glen Blvd., Los Angeles, CA 90077. Ray and Nancy Avery buy and sell entire collections and rare single 78s, LPs, transcriptions, CDs and jazz/big band photos.

RAY ANTHONY'S BIG BAND LIBRARY, 9288 Kinglet Dr., Los Angeles, CA 90069.

SERENDIPITY RECORDS, 4775 Durham Road, T. #77, Guilford, CT 06437-3607, telephone (203) 457-1039. Call or write for large catalog ($2.00).

TOWNHALL and SHEFFIELD LAB RECORDS, PO Box 5332, Santa Barbara, CA 93108. Harry James' last records, Pat Longo Big Band, others.

BOOKS

Basie, Count. *GOOD MORNING BLUES, THE AUTOBIOG-RAPHY OF COUNT BASIE*, as told to Albert Murray. Primus.

Bergreen, Laurence. *AS THOUSANDS CHEER: THE LIFE OF IRVING BERLIN.* Viking Press.

Collier, James Lincoln. *BENNY GOODMAN AND THE SWING ERA.* Oxford University Press.

Hall, Fred. *DIALOGUES IN SWING* (previous volume to this one). Pathfinder Publishing of California, 458 Dorothy Ave., Ventura, CA 93003.

Klauber, Bruce H. *WORLD OF GENE KRUPA.* Introduction by Mel Torme, Pathfinder Publishing of California, 458 Dorothy Ave., Ventura, CA 93003.

Lees, Gene; Dennys, Lester & Orpen. *OSCAR PETERSON: THE WILL TO SWING.* Also *MEET ME AT JIM AND ANDY'S, SINGERS AND THE SONG, WAITING FOR DIZZY* (all originally in Gene Lee's JAZZLETTER), and *INVENT-ING CHAMPAGNE, THE STORY OF LERNER AND LOWE*, all by Gene Lees, all Oxford University Press. Available in stores and also direct from Lees at PO Box 240, Ojai, CA 93024.

Rey, Luise King. *THE SINGING KINGS* and *THE SWINGING YEARS.* Order direct from Luise and Alvino Rey, PO Box 321, Sandy, Utah 84070.

Simon, George T. *THE BIG BANDS.* Collier Books. Arthur Newman Jazz Books.

Torme, Mel. *TRAPS, THE DRUM WONDER: THE STORY OF BUDDY RICH.* Oxford University Press (available September 1991).

Walker, Leo. *THE BIG BAND ALMANAC.* Order direct from Leo Walker, 6209 McKellips Rd., Palmas del Sol, Mesa, AZ 85206.

DISCOGRAPHY

STEVE ALLEN

ALL-STAR JAZZ CONCERT, VOL. I & II. (JASMINE – MCA) (LP)

INTRODUCING ANN JILLIAN, THE SINGER (ALL ALLEN SONGS) LAUREL

BIG BAND JAZZ BY RAY ANTHONY (ALL ALLEN SONGS) AEROSPACE (LP)

STEVE ALLEN has many of his earlier recordings, including vocals and piano solos available direct from him at 15201 BURBANK, VAN NUYS, CA 91401.

COUNT BASIE

COUNT BASIE AND THE KANSAS CITY 7 (MCA/IMPULSE)

APRIL IN PARIS (VERVE)

BASIE JAM (No. 1, 2 & 3) (PABLO)

THE BEST OF COUNT BASIE (MCA)

THE ESSENTIAL COUNT BASIE, Vol. 1, 2 & 3) (COLUMBIA)

FOR THE FIRST TIME (Basie/Ray Brown, Louis Bellson) (PABLO)

BRAND NEW WAGON: COUNT BASIE, 1947 (RCA BLUEBIRD)

COUNT BASIE AND JOE WILLIAMS (VERVE)

COUNT BASIE AND THE MILLS BROTHERS (MCA)

COUNT BASIE AND FRANK SINATRA (REPRISE)

COUNT BASIE AND TONY BENNETT (COLUMBIA)

BIG BAND BASH: BASIE AND BENNETT (INTERMEDIA)

HOW ABOUT THIS: KAY STARR AND COUNT BASIE (PARAMOUNT)

TONY BENNETT

ALL TIME GREATEST HITs (COLUMBIA)

THE ART OF EXCELLENCE (COLUMBIA)

ASTORIA (portrait Of An Artist) (COLUMBIA)

BENNETT AND BERLIN (COLUMBIA)

AT CARNEGIE HALL (COLUMBIA)

I LEFT MY HEART IN SAN FRANCISCO (COLUMBIA)

THE MOVIE SONG ALBUM (COLUMBIA)

TONY BENNETT JAZZ (COLUMBIA)

TONY BENNETT AND BILL EVANS (FANTASY)

THE SPECIAL MAGIC OF TONY BENNETT (DRG)

BENNETT AND BASIE (INTERMEDIA AND (DIFFERENT CUTS) COLUMBIA)

LES BROWN

BEST OF THE BIG BANDS: LES BROWN (COLUMBIA)

BEST OF THE BIG BANDS: DORIS DAY AND LES BROWN (COLUMBIA)

ANYTHING GOES (1990 RECORDINGS) (USA)

DIGITAL SWING (1986 RECORDINGS) (FANTASY)

THE BEST OF LES BROWN (MCA)

THE LES BROWN STORY (CAPITOL)

LES BROWN: 1944-1957 (FOUR VOLUMES)(HINDSIGHT)(LP)

SENTIMENTAL JOURNEY (VERVE)

LES BROWN PLAYS SOUTH PACIFIC (CAPITOL/ENGLAND)

CONCERT AT THE PALLADIUM (JASMINE)(LP)

SYMPHONIC SUITES FOR TWO BANDS WITH VIC SCHOEN (MCA)(LP)

DUKE ELLINGTON

THE BLANTON-WEBSTER BAND: ELLINGTON 1939-1942 (RCA BLUEBIRD)(CD, LP, CASSETTES)

BLACK, BROWN AND BEIGE: ELLINGTON 1944-1946 (RCA BLUEBIRD)(CD, LP, CASSETTES)

AND HIS MOTHER CALLED HIM BILL: ELLINGTON 1967 (RCA BLUEBIRD)

THE BEST OF DUKE ELLINGTON (CAPITOL)

BLUES IN ORBIT (COLUMBIA)

ELLINGTON INDIGOS (COLUMBIA)

COLUMBIA JAZZ MASTERPIECES (COLUMBIA)

DUKE ELLINGTON WORLD BROADCASTING SERIES (NINE LPs)(CIRCLE)

22 ORIGINAL BIG BAND RECORDINGS (HINDSIGHT)

SUCH SWEET THUNDER (COLUMBIA)

MUSIC IS MY MISTRESS (1989: MERCER ELLINGTON CONDUCTS)(MUSICMASTERS)

DUKE ELLINGTON AND COUNT BASIC: FIRST TIME! (COLUMBIA)

FRANCIS A. AND EDWARD K. (SINATRA AND ELLINGTON)(REPRISE)

HELEN FORREST

ON THE SUNNY SIDE OF THE STREET: WITH CARMEN DRAGON ORCHESTRA (AUDIOPHILE)

HELEN FORREST AND DICK HAYMES (MCA)

NOW AND FOREVER (1983 RECORDINGS)(STASH)

ALSO: WITH HARRY JAMES (COLUMBIA, CAPITOL, HINDSIGHT) BENNY GOODMAN (COLUMBIA)

AND ARTIE SHAW (RCA VICTOR AND RCA BLUEBIRD)

JOHNNY GREEN

STARRING FRED ASTAIRE (COLUMBIA)(LP)

AN AMERICAN IN PARIS (CBS)

HARRY JAMES

THE SHEFFIELD SESSIONS: 1974-1979 (3 DISC CD)(SHEFFIELD LAB)

BEST OF THE BIG BANDS: HARRY JAMES WITH HELEN FORREST, KITTY KALLEN (COL.)

WILLIE SMITH WITH THE HARRY JAMES ORCHESTRA (CO-LUMBIA)

COMPACT JAZZ: HARRY JAMES (VERVE)

THE GOLDEN TRUMPET OF HARRY JAMES (LONDON)

HARRY JAMES' GREATEST HITS WITH FRANK SINATRA, HELEN FORREST, DICK HAYMES (COL.) HITS OF HARRY JAMES (CAPITOL)

HARRY JAMES 1943-1949 (6 LPs)(HINDSIGHT)

HARRY JAMES AND DICK HAYMES (CIRCLE)(LP)

CRAZY RHYTHM (VERVE)

HARRY JAMES 1954 (CIRCLE)

COMIN' FROM A GOOD PLACE (DIRECT-TO-DISC)(SHEFFIELD LAB)

THE KING JAMES VERSION (DIRECT-TO-DISC)(SHEFFIELD LAB)

STILL HARRY AFTER ALL THESE YEARS (DIRECT-TO-DISC)(SHEFFIELD LAB)

HERB JEFFRIES

WITH DUKE ELLINGTON: THE BLANTON-WEBSTER BAND (RCA BLUEBIRD)(CD, LP, CASSETTES)

I GOT THE WORLD ON A STRING (SIGNATURE)

Other Jeffries' records available direct from him at 12751 MAGNOLIA BLVD., NORTH HOLLYWOOD, CA 91607.

THE KING SISTERS WITH ALVINO REY

Large selection available through:

ALVINO REY, P. O. BOX 321, SANDY, UT 84091

KAY STARR

KAY STARR'S AGAIN! (CAPITOL)

KAY STARR IN THE 1940s (HINDSIGHT)(LP)

KAY STARR WITH LES PAUL, JOE VENUTI & BILLY BUTTERFIELD (HINDSIGHT)(LP)

Resources

KAY STARR ON BROADWAY (CAPITOL-JAPAN)(LP)

KAY STARR WITH COUNT BASIE (PARAMOUNT)(LP)

TEDDY WILSON

TEDDY WILSON AND HIS ALL-STARS (MUSICRAFT)

WITH BILLIE IN MIND (CHIAROSCURO)

AS TIME GOES BY (MUSICRAFT)

TEDDY WILSON: JAZZ ARCHIVES

TEDDY WILSON TRIO IN EUROPE (FANTASY)

THE COMPLETE BENNY GOODMAN (Vol. 1 through 8)(RCA-BLUEBIRD)

TOGETHER AGAIN (WITH GENE KRUPA, BENNY GOODMAN, LIONEL HAMPTON)(RCA-BLUEBIRD)

THE BENNY GOODMAN SEXTETS (COLUMBIA)

SLIPPED DISC: THE BENNY GOODMAN SEXTET (COLUMBIA)

LIVE AT CARNEGIE HALL (GOODMAN CONCERT)(COLUMBIA)

BENNY GOODMAN: AIRPLAY (SIGNATURE)

THE QUINTESSENTIAL BILLIE HOLIDAY (Vol. 1 through 6)(COLUMBIA)

Also look for coming reissues on COLUMBIA, COMMODORE and VERVE.

INDEX

Resources

228

Resources

230

ORDER FORM

Pathfinder Publishing of California
458 Dorothy Ave.
Ventura, CA 93003
Telephone (805) 642-9278   FAX (805) 650-3656

Please send me the following books from Pathfinder Publishing:

_____ Copies of **Agony & Death on a**
          Gold Rush Steamer @ $8.95 $_____

_____ Copies of **Beyond Sympathy** @ $9.95 $_____

_____ Copies of **Dialogues In Swing** @ $12.95 $_____

_____ Copies of **Let Your Ideas Speak Out** @ **$8.95** $_____

_____ Copies of **Living Creatively**
          With Chronic Illness @ $11.95 $_____

_____ Copies of **More Dialogues In Swing**
          Softcover @ $14.95 $_____
          Hardcover @ $22.95 $_____

_____ Copies of **No Time For Goodbyes** @ $8.95 $_____

_____ Copies of **Marlin Justice** Soft Cover @ $9.95 $_____

_____ Copies of **Marlin Justice** Hard Cover @ $16.95 $_____

_____ Copies of **Quest For Respect** @ $6.95 $_____

_____ Copies of **Stop Justice Abuse** @ $10.95 $_____

_____ Copies of **Surviving a Japanese POW Camp**
          @ $11.95 $_____

_____ Copies of **Shipwrecks, Smugglers & Maritime**
Mysteries @ $9.95 $_____

_____ Copies of **World of Gene Krupa** @ $14.95 $_____

_____ Copies of **Chart/Maps** @ $3.95

    Title_____ $_____

                           Sub-Total $_____

    Californians: Please add 6.00% tax. $_____

    Shipping* $_____

                   Grand Total $_____

I understand that I may return the book for a full refund if not satisfied.

Name:_____

Address:_____
_____ZIP:_____

*SHIPPING CHARGES U.S.
Books: Enclose $2.50 for the first book and .50c for each additional book. UPS: Truck; $3.50 for first item, .50c for each additional. UPS Air: $5.00 for first item, $1.50 for each additional item. Maps: $2.50 for the first 6 maps, and .50c for each additional 6 maps.

231